CONTENTS

Music and Entertainment

100 THINGS TO DO IN GAINESVILLE BEFORE YOU DIE

LAUREN GONZALEZ

Reedy Press
PO Box 5131
St. Louis, MO 63139, USA
reedypress.com

Library of Congress Control Number: 2024939320

ISBN: 9781681065359

Design by Jill Halpin

All photos are courtesy of Lauren Gonzalez.

Printed in the United States of America
24 25 26 27 28   5 4 3 2 1

100 THINGS TO DO IN GAINESVILLE BEFORE YOU DIE

See a massive live oak tree at Cellon Oak Park.

Sports and Recreation

Culture and History

Shopping and Fashion

Step into a plant-lovers paradise
at Serpentine Plants + Provisions.

Walk to the Century Tower on the University of Florida campus.

ACKNOWLEDGMENTS

Thank you to all my wonderful family and friends for your help in making this book happen, for making suggestions, and for coming with me on countless day trips to explore.

To my husband Juan, thank you for being my forever adventure partner and supporting every crazy idea I have.

To my parents, Jim and Deb, thank you for always encouraging me to pursue my dreams and offering unwavering support along the way. And for instilling in me a sense of adventure and a love of nature that I now get to share with others.

To every single local business owner, artisan, vendor, restaurateur, park manager, advocate, historian, event organizer, and entrepreneur, there would be no book without you. You've poured your heart and soul into this community and made Gainesville a truly special place to live.

To my Florida Lives followers and community, thank you for supporting me in my journey as an online creator and for your invaluable comments, suggestions, and feedback. Without you, I would not have had the opportunity to write this book.

PREFACE

My family moved to Gainesville when I was 9 years old. Back then, it may have been easily written off as just the "home of the Florida Gators." Now, 20 years later, Gainesville is a dynamic city filled with a vibrant local community, natural wonders, foodie gems, annual festivals, and plenty of things to do.

Alachua County's slogan, "Where nature and culture meet," certainly rings true for Gainesville. An abundance of parks, lakes, and trails are accentuated with Old Florida charm and history everywhere you look. The sprawling University of Florida campus is a beautiful historic backdrop for a vibrant downtown full of live music, unique bars and eateries, festivals, and a thriving arts scene. Gainesville's incredible sense of community has allowed many local and family-owned shops, restaurants, breweries, and coffee shops to flourish here in recent years, with more popping up all the time.

For temporary Gainesville residents—students and faculty who plan to stay only a few years—this book will be your guide as you explore your new city. For lifelong residents, I'm willing to bet even you will discover something new in this book. I know I did while doing my research. There's so much history and culture in Gainesville you may never have known, even if you've driven by a place hundreds of times.

Although there are certainly many more than 100 things to do in Gainesville, I hope you will use this book as a jumping-off point for some incredible adventures. Whether you're looking for adrenaline-filled day trips, a romantic spot for date night, or a weekend activity for the kids, this book has something for everyone.

Keep in touch with me on Facebook and Instagram @100ThingsGNV for more pictures, stories, and adventures in Gainesville. Hope to see you around town soon!

—Lauren Gonzalez

Have a slice of pizza and enjoy the eclectic vibes at Satchel's.

FOOD AND DRINK

1

TRY A CHICKEN SANDWICH

AT GERMAIN'S CHICKEN SANDWICHES

Frequently recognized as one of the best chicken sandwiches in Gainesville, Germain's is definitely worth the hype. Their sandwiches are everything you could want—hot, crispy, juicy, and incredibly delicious. From classic flavors to innovative creations, each sandwich at Germain's is crafted with care into a mouthwatering masterpiece. The house-made sauces, pickles, and unique flavor combinations make Germain's menu stand out. Each sandwich comes with amazing ranch-seasoned crispy french fries, but I also recommend getting a bowl of the exceptional Brussel Caesar Salad to share. On top of all that, they also serve local beers, specialty wines, and house-made drinks and cocktails. Plus, they have several plant-based and gluten-free options available. The restaurant itself has great laid-back vibes with friendly service, vibrant decor, and indoor and outdoor seating.

220 NW 8th Ave., Ste. 10, 352-554-4545
germainsgnv.com

2

GRAB A SLICE
AT SATCHEL'S PIZZA

Perhaps the most iconic restaurant in town, Satchel's Pizza has been a favorite eatery since 2003. This eclectic café is not only fun to look at, but it also serves up some incredible pizza. The decor is funky, colorful, and nostalgic, with recycled materials making up many of the art installations. Basically everything at Satchel's is house-made, from the pizza dough to the sodas to the famous salad dressing. Of course, the pizza is undeniably delicious, with more than 30 traditional and unique toppings to choose from. Satchel's can even whip up vegan and gluten-sensitive pies. My go-to order? Bacon, pineapple, and black olives with plenty of Tammy Ranch on the side. For a one-of-a-kind dining experience, eat at the booth in the vintage van! Go during the week to snag the van seating with little or no wait. Don't forget to stop by Lightnin' Salvage behind the restaurant for unique gifts, a bar, and live music. Satchel's Pizza is closed Sundays and Mondays.

1800 NE 23rd Ave., 352-335-7272
satchelspizza.com

3

SIP A CRAFT BREW
AT SWAMP HEAD BREWERY

Gainesville is home to a flourishing craft beer scene, and each of the breweries in town brings its own unique flavor to the table. Whether you're into hoppy IPAs, rich stouts, or nonalcoholic options, there's something for everyone at Gainesville's breweries. Swamp Head Brewery combines great beer and a unique atmosphere. It has a big outdoor space situated next to a pond and cypress trees, giving it a swamp-like vibe. It's the perfect place to enjoy a laid-back drink with a group. Swamp Head has a large and ever-changing selection of craft brews available in their cozy (and dog-friendly) wetlands taproom. The brewery often hosts food trucks, live music, and special events for a fun experience at every visit. Whether you're a beer connoisseur or a casual enthusiast, you'll be sure to find a new favorite at Swamp Head Brewery.

3650 SW 42nd Ave., 352-505-3035
swamphead.com

4

GET A FRESHLY BAKED CROISSANT FROM UPPERCRUST

If you're looking for a wide selection of unique baked goods in Gainesville, look no further than Uppercrust. They've been serving up homemade pastries, breads, cakes, and more in Gainesville for over 40 years. Founded in 1981 and inspired by European bakeries, Uppercrust is perhaps most well-known for their croissants. With an experienced designated croissantier (yes, that's their actual title), you know a whole lotta love and care is put into making those delicious buttery pastry treats. In addition to delightful baked goods and coffee, the original shop in northwest Gainesville, aka Mothercrust, also stocks a curated selection of wine, stationery, gifts, and specialty foods. Petit Uppercrust is the bakery's newest location in Haile Plantation, serving up a smaller-scale selection of favorites. You also can regularly find Uppercrust at the weekly Haile Village Farmers Market.

Mothercrust (NW)
4118 NW 16th Blvd., 352-376-7187

Petite Uppercrust (Haile)
8766 SW 27th Ln., 352-554-5096

uppercrustgnv.com

INDULGE IN A STEAK
AT EMBERS

Head to Embers Wood Fire Grill for an elegant dining experience at one of Gainesville's premier steak houses. From the moment you step inside, you'll be surrounded by an air of sophistication and coziness, setting the stage for an excellent evening. The Embers menu is crafted to perfection, featuring a selection of prime cuts of beef, pasta, fresh seafood, appetizers, and indulgent desserts. Pair your dinner with a bottle of wine from the extensive selection with help from expert sommeliers. Great service, an inviting atmosphere, and quality ingredients set Embers apart. On nice evenings, you can sit outside in the patio garden to enjoy your meal. Whether you're celebrating a birthday or graduation, or just having a nice night on the town, Embers is worth the visit. It's open Monday through Saturday starting at 5 p.m. Reservations are strongly recommended.

3545 SW 34th St., Ste. A, 352-380-0901
embersofflorida.com

6

SHOW YOUR GATOR SPIRIT
AT THE SWAMP RESTAURANT

The Swamp Restaurant is a Gainesville staple near the University of Florida campus. Since its founding in 1994, the Swamp has been a favorite gathering place for locals and students, offering a sports bar vibe and lively atmosphere. The restaurant temporarily closed between 2020 and 2022 but reopened in a new location nearby, recreating the likeness of the historic building. The Swamp's welcoming neighborhood ambiance extends into multiple dining areas with a spacious outdoor lawn and rooftop seating. The menu features a variety of classic dishes like burgers, sandwiches, salads, and wings, plus a special menu for game days. The Swamp is well known as a popular spot for cheering on the Florida Gators on game day. The restaurant features multiple large-screen TVs throughout the dining area so you won't miss your favorite game. The Swamp is the perfect spot to enjoy a casual meal, catch up with friends over drinks, or cheer on your team.

1104 SW 2nd Ave., 352-377-9267
swamprestaurant.com

7

SHOP FRESH
AT WARD'S SUPERMARKET

Ward's Supermarket is a local, family-owned grocery store that has been serving the Gainesville community since 1951. Ward's is known for its commitment to supplying fresh, quality products that are sourced locally whenever possible. In addition to standard supermarket goods, Ward's offers an extensive selection of farm-fresh produce, including many organic options. Ward's is also well known for its high-quality meats and wide range of cuts. In-store butchers can help make suggestions and custom cut your order. Ward's also offers specialty goods, such as health care products, local wine and beer, and unique products you can't find anywhere else. The bulk goods selection, including nuts, grains, baking supplies, and herbs, allows you to shop sustainably. Ward's Supermarket has earned a loyal customer base over the years by treating shoppers like family, and it continues to offer some fantastic local and natural products to the community.

515 NW 23rd Ave., 352-372-1741
wardsgainesville.com

8

TRY SOMETHING NEW
AT THE TOP

The Top in downtown Gainesville is consistently named as one of the best restaurants in town. Known for its eclectic atmosphere, delicious food, and fun cocktails, The Top has been a beloved dining spot in Gainesville for years. With a ton of options on the menu, there's always something unique to try, like comfort food classics with a twist and creative weekly specials. Plus, they've got great options for those looking for vegetarian, vegan, or gluten-free meals. In addition to the food, The Top is well known for its lively bar, featuring an extensive selection of craft beers, cocktails, and wines. The Top has a unique ambiance with funky decor, vintage furnishings, and fun artwork on the walls. The restaurant's laid-back vibe and welcoming atmosphere make it a favorite local spot to gather and enjoy great food and drinks. The Top is open Tuesday through Sunday from 5 p.m. to 2 a.m., with late-night bar food being offered after dinner hours.

30 N Main St., 352-337-1188
thetophub.com

TIP

After your meal, make your way across the street to the Arcade Bar to enjoy games, drinks, and some friendly competition. Three floors of games, two full bars, and a fun atmosphere make the Arcade Bar well worth the stop. With all kinds of games from pinball and arcade classics to Mario Kart and Skee-Ball. Open daily from 5 p.m. to 1:45 a.m., and open to ages 21 and up only after 8 p.m.

6 E University Ave.
thearcadeplex.com

9

STEP INTO A FRENCH BISTRO

AT ALPIN

For a trip to a cozy French bistro without a passport, Alpin Bistro is a must-visit in downtown Gainesville. As a French family owned bistro, their menu is filled with classic French dishes like croque monsieur, quiche, and French onion soup. Creative specials du jour ensure plenty of options to try each time you visit. Everything is made fresh using high-quality, local ingredients and specially curated, imported goods. Plus, there are great vegetarian and gluten-free options. I recommend indulging in one of the decadent croques and enjoying a glass or two of wine. Alpin Bistro is the perfect intimate setting for a date night, a special girls' night out, or any occasion that calls for a relaxed evening of delicious food and drink. A charming garden patio even offers outdoor seating. Alpin Bistro is open Tuesday through Saturday for dinner plus Saturday brunch and is closed on Sundays and Mondays.

15 SW 2nd St., 352-204-2873
alpinbistro.com

10

SAMPLE DIFFERENT CUISINES

AT 4TH AVE FOOD PARK

Food parks are fun dining destinations that feature a variety of food vendors in one location, allowing visitors to enjoy multiple cuisines in a shared dining space. 4th Ave Food Park has several local food vendors, including SquareHouse Pizza, the Opus Coffee Airstream, Muñecas Taco Garden, Humble Wood Fire Bagels, and others. The outdoor seating area and patio spaces allow everyone in your group to grab something different while still getting to eat together. Anybody can find something to enjoy at 4th Ave Food Park, with many vendors serving gluten-free and vegan options. The park-like courtyard has plenty of room for kids to run around while adults hang out. Murals and eclectic decor liven up the space for an all-around great experience. With community events like workshops, live music, and markets, a trip to 4th Ave Food Park can be for more than just good food!

409 SW 4th Ave.
4thavefoodpark.com

11

SAVOR AUTHENTIC FLAVORS
AT MI APÁ LATIN CAFÉ

For a taste of authentic Cuban food, head to one of four Mi Apá locations in Alachua County. A Gainesville favorite for over two decades, Mi Apá serves Cuban sandwiches, hearty entrées, cafe con leche, and much more. The vibrant, tropical atmosphere, especially in the Jonesville location, is the perfect backdrop for a tasty breakfast, lunch, or dinner. Some of my favorite things to order are the empanadas, papas rellenas (fried stuffed potatoes), and arroz con pollo (chicken with yellow rice). If you're on the University of Florida campus, there's a quick-service Mi Apá in the Reitz Union Food Court. The other locations offer options to dine in, order takeout, or make a quick stop through the drive-through. The newest location in Jonesville also has a private event space that can seat up to 30 people.

Reitz Union Food Court, Reitz Union Dr., Floor 1
114 SW 34th St., 352-376-7020
14209 W Newberry Rd., Ste. B, Newberry, 352-545-4430
15634 NW US Hwy. 441, Ste. F, Alachua, 386-418-0838
miapalatincafe.com

ADMIRE THE MEMORABILIA
AT SPURRIER'S GRIDIRON GRILLE

Experience the legacy of former Florida Gators quarterback and coach Steve Spurrier at Spurrier's Gridiron Grille in Celebration Pointe. This part restaurant, part museum features elevated American favorites on the menu and walls lined with college football memorabilia. Photos, trivia tidbits, and quotes from Coach Spurrier are peppered all throughout the restaurant. Dine inside, head to the patio, or check out Visors Rooftop to enjoy your food with a view. You'll definitely want to try a specialty cocktail or a craft beer—Spurrier's has three house beers on tap brewed in partnership with First Magnitude Brewing Company. With three bars and multiple TVs broadcasting all the top games, this is a great place to spend a game day, or any day, soaking in the spirited atmosphere. Reservations are highly encouraged for dinner and the weekend brunch buffet.

4860 Steve Spurrier Way, 352-500-4422
spurriers.com

13

UNWIND
AT SUPERETTE

Discover a mecca of fine wines, delicious flavors, and impeccable vibes at superette. Step into this inviting bistro and wine bar and let the relaxation begin. With its lovingly curated selection of wines from around the globe, superette offers something to satisfy every palate and occasion. You can savor wine by the glass or bottle, and there are great weekday happy hour specials. When dining here, indulge in Mediterranean fare, sandwiches, and small plates. Or complement your wine with a curated assortment of gourmet cheeses, charcuterie, and other artisanal delights. Enjoy the vibes in the indoor space or check out the extensive seating in the courtyard. Wine tastings are offered every Thursday from 6 to 8 p.m., when you can sample four wines of the week. Superette has a great cozy and intimate atmosphere for any occasion, from a group evening out, a date night, or a weekend brunch. And who doesn't love wine and cheese?

1511 NW 2nd St., 352-451-4144
superettegnv.com

TAKE A COOKING CLASS
AT THE FAT TUSCAN

A cooking class at The Fat Tuscan promises a flavorful journey of Italian cuisine. Inside the warm and inviting historic home-turned-culinary venue, participants learn under the tutelage of chef and owner Michelle Gioviti and experienced chefs. The classes are designed to be an immersive experience, allowing you to cook alongside the pros while honing techniques and learning more about traditional Italian flavors. Multiple classes are offered on days, evenings, weekdays, and weekends. You can learn about everything from making fresh pasta to baking pastries to pairing wine with a gourmet dinner. Both novice and experienced cooks will enjoy the welcoming, hands-on experience of a cooking class at The Fat Tuscan. There are even specific cooking classes for couples that include a full dinner. In addition to classes, The Fat Tuscan also offers event space for intimate gatherings such as private dinners, showers, and small weddings. You also can shop for Italian wines and freshly made gourmet gift baskets.

725 NE 1st St., 352-505-5648
fattuscan.com

HAVE HIGH TEA
AT TEATIME TRANQUILITY & TREASURES

This charming tearoom is located in a historic building in Alachua. Guests can indulge in a pot of warm tea, served with a teacup, accompanied by sweet and savory treats. Choose from a carefully curated selection of teas, from oolong to black, with a new special every day. The attention to detail in both the decor and the presentation of the tea adds to the overall charm of this spot. Many of the teacups and teapots in the tearoom are for sale, along with the antiques in the boutique upstairs. One of the most popular offerings at Teatime Tranquility & Treasures is the high tea service, where you can enjoy teas and courses of delightful pastries, sandwiches, and scones. Make sure to call for a reservation for high tea at least 24 hours in advance. This historic locale is also available as a wedding or event venue, complete with a beautiful garden and gazebo.

14603 Main St., Alachua, 386-243-9199
teatimetranquility.com

DINE WITH A VIEW
AT CHOPSTIX

Treat yourself to a rare waterfront dining experience in Gainesville at Chopstix Cafe. This family owned restaurant offers a variety of pan-Asian dishes that are sure to delight your taste buds. Dining on the patio is a must, and if you can time your visit just right, there's nothing like watching the sunset over the water while enjoying a cold beverage and a spectacular meal. Chopstix has something for every palate, from savory stir-fries and sushi rolls to seafood dishes and curries. They are widely known for creating custom dishes on request, adjusting spice and flavor levels, and catering to those with dietary restrictions. Chopstix is an amazing dining experience for a relaxing evening out with friends or loved ones. Chopstix is closed on Sundays and Mondays.

3500 SW 13th St., 352-367-0003

17

RISE AND SHINE
AT DAYLIGHT DONUTS

Daylight Donuts is a beloved bakery known for its delicious assortment of freshly made doughnuts and baked goods. This locally owned and operated shop has been serving mouthwatering treats to the Gainesville community for years. From classic glazed doughnuts to specialty flavors like maple bacon and red velvet, there's something to satisfy every craving. You even can get your doughnuts custom-made with your choice of 10 fillings. In addition to their doughnuts, Daylight Donuts also offers a variety of pastries, kolaches, and breakfast sandwiches, making it a great spot to grab a quick bite on the go or to indulge in a morning treat. For the best selection of doughnuts, head to the store earlier in the day. Daylight Donuts is open Monday through Saturday from 5 a.m. to 12:30 p.m.

1109 N Main St., 352-367-8409
gainesvilledonut.com

GET CAFFEINATED
AT COFFEE CULTURE

Discover the inviting atmosphere and tasty drinks waiting for you at Coffee Culture, nestled in the heart of the Northwest. The menu is full of specialty espresso and coffee drinks, from smooth lattes to robust espressos and refreshing cold brews. A number of unique flavored syrups allow you to enjoy your coffee with customized flavor. Pair your beverage with a delicious sweet or savory pastry, baked in-house, to complement the rich flavors of the coffee. There are plenty of tables inside and outside, plus parking is available. If you're on the go, swing by the drive-through for a quick pick-me-up. For a spot to catch up with friends or a place to get some work done with an excellent coffee, Coffee Culture is one of the best!

2020 NW 13th St., 352-377-1700
facebook.com/coffeeculturegvl

19

INDULGE IN ITALIAN FAVORITES
AT PIESANOS STONE FIRED PIZZA

Savor the flavors of Italian cuisine at Piesanos, where fresh ingredients shine in every bite. Traditional pasta dishes and delicious stone-fired pizzas are the stars of the menu, with appetizers, salads, and entrées providing plenty of variety. One of their most-loved dishes is the complimentary starter rolls. The fluffy rolls are bathed in their house Italian dressing, making them full of flavor and so craveable. Piesanos' cozy and welcoming atmosphere and friendly staff make you feel right at home. Now with 13 locations across Central Florida, including three in Gainesville, Piesanos is a regional favorite. So whether you're dining with family and friends, grabbing a quick bite, or ordering takeout for a cozy night in, Piesanos is a great option for fantastic Italian cuisine.

5200 NW 43rd St., Ste. 302, 352-371-7437
1250 W University Ave., 352-375-2337
5757 SW 75th St., Ste. 101, 352-371-8646
piesanostogo.com

PICK YOUR OWN BLUEBERRIES
AT AMBER BROOKE FARMS

Blueberry picking at Amber Brooke Farms is a delightful family-friendly activity. The farm is less than 30 minutes outside of Gainesville in Williston. During the blueberry U-Pick season, typically March through May, Amber Brooke Farms opens its fields to the public to pick their own berries. Take a bucket and enjoy a stroll through the rows of different varieties of berries. Make sure to sample some of each to find your favorite variety! Blueberries are one of the easiest fruits to pick because the fruit grows at all heights, so the littlest to the tallest members of your group won't have to reach up high or stoop down low. When blueberries are ripe, they will fall off in your hand—no cutting or pulling involved. Throughout the year, Amber Brooke Farms also offers U-Pick strawberries, peaches, sunflowers, zinnias, and more. They also host seasonal events like a strawberry festival and food and wine festival with entertainment and activities.

3250 NE 140th Ave., Williston, 352-638-7849
amberbrookefarms.com

21

DINE AND SHOP AT LA TIENDA

La Tienda, meaning "the store" in Spanish, is a popular Mexican restaurant and market offering a variety of authentic Mexican dishes and products. With delicious cuisine and big portions, it's easy to see why La Tienda is often named as one of the best Mexican restaurants in Gainesville. This casual counter-service spot serves up all the traditional favorites like chips and queso, enchiladas, and tacos. One of the most-loved dishes is the birria taco, a delicious and juicy beef taco with a broth for dipping. In the market section, you'll find a wide variety of products, from fresh tortillas and traditional spices to specialty snacks and beverages. There's also fresh meat and produce to help bring the authentic flavors to your own home. La Tienda is open daily for lunch and dinner.

2204 SW 13th St., 352-367-0022
latiendagnv.com

FIND A NEW FAVORITE

AT TIPPLE'S BREWS & WINE

Tipple's Brews & Wine is the perfect place to try a wide selection of craft beers and wines. As both a retail shop and tasting room, this unique concept allows you to purchase drinks by the can or glass at retail cost. There's a wide range of ever-changing craft beers, including local and international brews, plus a curated wine collection. There's something for every palate on the beer wall, from hoppy IPAs to fruity sours. The welcoming and laid-back atmosphere at Tipple's is great for a small gathering or watching the game. The knowledgeable staff can provide recommendations to help customers explore new and exciting beverages. Food trucks are sometimes found outside to have a bite to eat while you enjoy your beverage. Whether you're looking for a unique craft beer to enjoy at the cozy tasting bar or want to take home a bottle of fine wine for a special occasion, Tipple's Brews & Wine is a go-to spot.

2440 SW 76th St., Ste. 110, 352-672-6303
tipplesbrews.com

See thousands of bats fly overhead at the UF Bat Houses.

MUSIC
AND ENTERTAINMENT

23

SEE WHAT'S HAPPENING
AT BO DIDDLEY PLAZA

Bo Diddley Plaza is a mainstay public space that pays homage to the legendary Rock & Roll and Blues Hall of Famer Bo Diddley, who called Gainesville home for part of his life. The plaza serves as a musical and cultural hub in the heart of downtown, offering a venue for community events, festivals, and concerts. With an open-air stage, green space, and restaurants all around, Bo Diddley Plaza provides a memorable location for all types of events. Live music performances, markets, and even fitness and dance classes are held at the plaza frequently. When exploring downtown Gainesville, it's definitely worth dropping by for a free yoga session, enjoying a coffee, or listening to live music at Bo Diddley Plaza. The Union Street Farmers Market is held here each Wednesday from 4 to 7 p.m. The Live and Local Concert Series offers free monthly performances. Free fitness classes are held at various times each Monday through Thursday.

111 E University Ave., 352-393-8202
gainesvillefl.gov/venues/bo-diddley-plaza

CATCH A CONCERT
AT HEARTWOOD SOUNDSTAGE

With multiple live music events each week, a recording studio, plus a farmers market, Heartwood Soundstage is an arts and entertainment hub in Gainesville. Featuring musicians from near and far, Heartwood Soundstage is a platform for both up-and-coming and well-known artists. The venue offers an intimate indoor space designed for optimal sound quality, while larger events have plenty of space on the outdoor stage. Conveniently situated near bars and local restaurants, attendees easily can grab food or a drink nearby. Depot Park, just across the street, provides an additional recreational space for those interested in enjoying a walk or hitting the playground before or after events. One of the most popular events held at Heartwood Soundstage is the annual Tom Petty Weekend. The three-day event in October pays homage to the legendary band Tom Petty and the Heartbreakers, adding a special touch to Gainesville's music scene.

619 S Main St., 352-448-4849
heartwoodsoundstage.com

25

EXPERIENCE THE MAGIC OF THEATER
AT THE HIPPODROME

Standing as the historic centerpiece in downtown Gainesville, The Hippodrome Theatre is not to be missed. Founded in 1972, The Hippodrome has evolved into a dynamic arts hub, featuring two main entertainment spaces: the Mainstage and the Cinema. The unique blend of theatrical performances, film screenings, historic architecture, and an art gallery makes The Hippodrome a cultural pillar in the Gainesville community. The building, a former post office and district courthouse, was built in 1911 and is on the National Register of Historic Places. The Greek Revival–style architecture and original fixtures add to the magical and inviting atmosphere. The Mainstage showcases a variety of live productions, including plays and musicals. Some performances appear year after year, such as the beloved classic *A Christmas Carol*. The Cinema, on the other hand, screens independent, foreign, and classic films multiple evenings each week. Beyond its entertainment offerings, The Hippodrome also offers classes and workshops, behind-the-scenes building tours, live music, and other community events.

25 SE 2nd Pl., 352-375-4477
thehipp.org

TIP

There are so many restaurants and bars around The Hippodrome in downtown Gainesville, you have a ton of choices for dinner or drinks. For the perfect dinner-and-a-show date night, make a reservation at Amelia's Italian Restaurant, right behind The Hippodrome. After the show, head to The Traveler, a cozy wine bar, for a nightcap.

Amelia's Italian Restaurant
235 S Main St., Ste. 107, 352-373-1919
ameliasgnv.com

The Traveler
101 SE 2nd Pl., Ste. 108, 352-757-2985
thetravelerbar.com

GO BATTY
AT THE UF BAT HOUSES

There's no experience quite like watching hundreds of thousands of bats fly over your head at dusk. Make your way to the University of Florida campus around sunset to observe this incredible sight. The UF Bat Houses are the largest occupied bat houses in the world, with an estimated 450,000 to 500,000 bats! To see the bats fly, arrive before sunset to find a spot to park and to stand. There's a parking lot adjacent to the houses. The houses are in a fenced field with a sidewalk and benches nearby to watch from. The bats usually emerge 15 to 20 minutes after sunset or even earlier in the spring and summer months. Keep in mind that high winds, heavy rain, or cold weather may keep the bats inside the houses for the evening. The bat houses are open for public viewing daily with no fees.

2664 Museum Rd.
floridamuseum.ufl.edu/bats

To learn more about bats, head to Lubee Bat Conservancy, a nonprofit organization dedicated to bat conservation, care, and education. You can schedule a private VIP tour to view the facility or visit during one of their events, like the annual Florida Bat Festival, a beloved family-friendly tradition held each fall.

1309 NW 192nd Ave., 352-485-1250
lubee.org

27

GET YOUR GAME ON
AT BRAGGING RIGHTS AMUSEMENTS

It's no secret that arcades are a great way to spend a hot or rainy day, or a fun evening out with friends and family. Bragging Rights allows you to experience all the fun of an arcade for just one flat entrance fee! Say goodbye to purchasing tokens or swiping cards for each game. With an eclectic collection of hundreds of games ranging from recent favorites to classic pinball machines, there's something for everyone. You could spend hours here checking out each game, trying to beat your high score, or watching pinball masters. There's a bar in the back with beer, wine, and canned beverages, plus pizza and snacks. An all-you-can-play wristband costs $25 for the whole day, and discounts are available for students, veterans, first responders, and on certain days and times.

113 NW 8th Ave., 352-281-6937
braggingrights.com

TIP

Take a game break by grabbing a quick meal nearby. Your all-you-can-play wristband allows you to come and go from the arcade all day long! Head to Germain's Chicken Sandwiches across the street. Or walk up or drive through Mac's Drive-Thru for one of Gainesville's favorite burgers.

Germain's Chicken Sandwiches
220 NW 8th Ave., Ste. 10, 352-554-4545
germainsgnv.com

Mac's Drive-Thru
129 NW 10th Ave., 352-378-9842
macs-drive-thru.com

28

REV UP EXCITEMENT
AT GATORNATIONALS

Gatornationals is a thrilling multiday drag race event that attracts racing enthusiasts from across the country. Held annually in March at the Gainesville Raceway, this spectacle is part of the National Hot Rod Association (NHRA) drag racing series. The traditional East Coast opener showcases professional drag racers competing in various categories. With the first event being held at the raceway in 1970, Gatornationals has a storied history and is known for being a record-breaking venue. From the stands, spectators will experience the roar of powerful engines on the strip. Anyone who is sensitive to loud noises may want to bring ear protection. With the electrifying atmosphere, the action-packed Gatornationals is a must-attend for anyone interested in motorsports. Tickets start at $25. The Gainesville Raceway also holds a variety of other racing events throughout the year.

11211 N County Rd. 225, 352-377-0046
gainesvilleraceway.com

TIP

Can't get enough of drag racing history? Head to the Don Garlits Museum of Drag Racing, just a quick drive away in Ocala. With more than 100 racing and antique cars on display, this museum showcases the history of the sport of drag racing and is also home to the International Drag Racing Hall of Fame. Considered the father of drag racing, "Big Daddy" Don Garlits pioneered many drag racing innovations and set countless records.

13700 SW 16th Ave., Ocala, 352-245-8661
garlits.com

GET MEDIEVAL
AT THE HOGGETOWN MEDIEVAL FAIRE

Hear ye, hear ye! Don your finest Renaissance attire and make your way to the Hoggetown Medieval Faire! This is an immersive festival that transports attendees back to medieval times. Held annually in January or February, the fair has brought the medieval world to life in Gainesville for the last 37 years. Elaborate reenactments, jousting tournaments, and lively performances await on multiple stages throughout the fair. The enchanting atmosphere allows attendees to spend the day in a world of fantasy. You can wander through the bustling marketplace filled with artisans and vendors showcasing handmade wares, medieval attire, and live demonstrations. Or head to the food court for classic fair food and, of course, giant turkey legs. The fair has changed locations throughout its run in Gainesville, but the tradition remains alive. The Hoggetowne Medieval Faire provides a family-friendly environment with enchanting sights, sounds, and tastes of the medieval world, making it a much-anticipated and beloved tradition in Gainesville.

hoggetownemedfaire.com

30

IMMERSE YOURSELF IN THE MUSIC

AT FEST

Fest is an annual three-day music festival held in downtown Gainesville. Known for its lineup of punk, indie, and alternative music, Fest attracts music lovers from across the country for a weekend of live performances and community camaraderie. Fest is held annually in late October or early November, always coinciding with the weekend the Florida Gators travel to Jacksonville to take on the Georgia Bulldogs. It takes place throughout multiple venues in downtown Gainesville, including bars, music venues, and outdoor stages, creating a vibrant atmosphere spanning blocks. With its inclusive and welcoming vibe, Fest has become a staple event in Gainesville's independent arts and music scene over the past 20 years. You need tickets to attend the event, and they typically go on sale each year in the spring—make sure to get them early because the prices do increase and they often sell out.

thefestfl.com

LOOK FOR STARS
AT THE UF OBSERVATORY

The University of Florida Teaching Observatory is a facility dedicated to astronomical research and education. The observatory houses a variety of telescopes and equipment used by university researchers and students, and on certain Friday nights, they offer free public open houses. Visitors of all ages can peer through the multiple telescopes and observe the wonders of the night sky. You'll be able to see things like the moon, planets, and stars with amazing clarity. Different astronomical objects will be observable at different times of the year. Public open-house events also can include displays of images and animations, videos, presentations, hands-on demonstrations, and a chance to ask questions. Public nights are held from 8:30 to 10 p.m. on Friday nights when UF classes are in session during the fall and spring semesters. These events are weather-dependent and are not offered when there is significant cloud coverage.

University of Florida campus, between the physics
and engineering buildings, 352-294-1870
astro.ufl.edu/outreach/teaching-public-observatory

Are you a space lover? Check out the Kika Silva Pla Planetarium at Santa Fe College for an amazing intergalactic experience. The dome theater has a vast library of planetarium shows and even musical experiences. It is open for public showings most Friday evenings and Saturday afternoons and evenings.

3000 NW 83rd St., Bldg. X-129, 352-395-5225
sfcollege.edu/planetarium

32

HANG OUT
AT THE BULL

If you're in the mood for a laid-back evening of live music, head over to The Bull in downtown. The Bull is a cozy bar and community hub where local musicians and artists showcase their talent. The welcoming atmosphere and eclectic vibe make for a great venue to grab a drink and enjoy a show. The Bull offers a variety of entertainment throughout the week, from acoustic guitar sets and live jazz music to open mic nights. They even have salsa and swing dancing evenings with group dancing and instruction. Local art is displayed throughout The Bull, and you can catch poetry readings and storytelling hours often. This intimate space offers a bar stocked with a rotating selection of wines and local craft beers on tap. The Bull is open every night of the week to hang out with good company and enjoy the music.

18 SW 1st Ave., 352-672-6266
thebull-gnv.com

33

TRY YOUR HAND AT AXE THROWING

AT THE HATCHETBURY

Unleash your inner lumberjack and try axe throwing at The Hatchetbury! Axe throwing is one of the latest crazes sweeping the nation, and for good reason. This one-of-a-kind experience offers thrills, laughter, and a great time with friends, family, or a date. All ages are welcome to participate. An "axe-pert" will give you a demonstration and teach you the basics of axe throwing before you get started. Perfect your technique, compete in fun games, and revel in the glory of hitting a bull's-eye. Serving a selection of beer and wine, The Hatchetbury is a great place for a night out on the town or a special occasion. You can bring in your own takeout to enjoy while you play, or hit one of the many downtown restaurants after your game. The Hatchetbury is open Wednesday through Sunday, and an online reservation is recommended to avoid potential wait time as a walk-in.

213 NW 8th Ave., 352-717-2937
thehatchetbury.com

EXPERIENCE THE DUELING PIANOS

AT THE KEYS

Known for its lively and tropical atmosphere, The Keys Grill & Piano Bar serves up dynamic entertainment, flavorful food, and tasty cocktails. Although this Celebration Pointe restaurant is worth a visit anytime, you won't want to miss the dueling piano performance each Friday and Saturday night at 9 p.m. Talented pianists engage in a musical battle, taking song requests from the audience and creating an electrifying atmosphere. Sing or dance along to your favorite songs while enjoying the island-inspired menu and fruity cocktails. With indoor and outdoor seating and bars, this is a great spot for a fun night out with friends, a celebration, or simply a memorable dining experience. They also serve brunch on Sundays with a mouthwatering menu and great drink specials. View their website for a list of upcoming performances.

4860 Celebration Pointe Ave., Ste. 30, 352-554-5104
thekeysgainesville.com

GET SPOOKED
AT NEWBERRY CORNFIELD MAZE

Are you ready to get lost in a corn maze and be chased by monsters with chain saws? This seasonal spooky activity is sure to get your heart racing! Typically open every September and October, the Newberry Cornfield Maze has been a staple fall pastime since 2004. Located just past Jonesville, you'll forget that you're only a few minutes outside of town when you enter the haunted farm. Favorite activities include the haunted hayride, the walk-through haunted house (which compares to some of the ones at the theme parks!), and of course, the corn maze. You also can enjoy a variety of fair-style foods. The Kids Play Area is family friendly and offers games, farm animals, and a playground. During the day, the corn maze is not haunted, making for a fun experience for all. Don't forget to grab your tickets online in advance to save time and money at the gate.

20015 W Newberry Rd., Newberry, 352-354-5118
newberrycornfieldmaze.com

TIP

For more seasonal farm fun, check out Kirby Family Farm in Williston. They offer holiday events throughout the year themed around riding their 1800s-era train around the property. All aboard the Rock-n-Roll Easter Train, the fall Scary Train, or the Christmas Train!

19650 NE 30th St., Williston, 352-812-7435
kirbyfarm.com

LISTEN TO THE MUSIC
AT ONE LOVE CAFE

One Love Cafe is a favorite local hangout that combines delicious food, a family-friendly atmosphere, and relaxed vibes. With a great live music lineup, this is the perfect place to enjoy a meal and listen to the music. The café offers a tasty menu focusing on fresh, locally sourced ingredients. From savory sandwiches and salads to curated specials, weekend brunch, and a full bar, One Love Cafe caters to a range of tastes. The outdoor seating area is surrounded by a park-like setting and features a large field and a community garden. Community events, such as karaoke nights, craft classes, and festivals, are frequently part of the events lineup. The café's commitment to sustainability and supporting local growers adds an extra layer of appeal. Whether you're looking for a casual brunch spot, an outdoor space to work with a cup of coffee, or a lively venue to enjoy an evening meal, One Love Cafe stands out as a must-try restaurant.

4989 NW 40th Pl., 352-509-3131
onelove.cafe

CELEBRATE SUMMER
AT THE NEWBERRY WATERMELON FESTIVAL

The Newberry Watermelon Festival is an annual celebration that pays tribute to one of the region's most beloved fruits. Typically held in late May, the festival brings the community together for a fun-filled day of activities, entertainment, and, of course, plenty of watermelon treats. The Newberry Watermelon Festival has been ongoing since 1946, making it one of the longest-running continuous festivals in the country. Festival attendees can enjoy a variety of family-friendly attractions, including live music performances, parades, art vendors, carnival games, and children's activities. One of the main highlights of the festival is the contests and competitions, such as seed-spitting contests, watermelon-eating contests, pageants, and the crowning of the festival's annual Watermelon Queen. And no watermelon festival would be complete without plenty of farm-fresh, juicy watermelon to enjoy. Festivalgoers can indulge in slices of locally grown watermelon, as well as a variety of watermelon-inspired dishes and beverages.

24850 SW 17th Pl., Newberry
newberrywatermelonfestival.com

38

BE ENTERTAINED
AT THE GAINESVILLE COMMUNITY PLAYHOUSE

In Gainesville, there are several venues that offer the entertaining experience of local theater. These spaces provide stages to showcase local talent and provide the community with access to performing arts. The Gainsville Community Playhouse performs a variety of shows, from comedies and musicals to well-known classics and everything in between. Founded in 1927, the Gainesville Community Playhouse is one of the oldest community theaters in Florida. Its current venue, the Vam York Theater, is an intimate venue that allows viewers to be up close to all the action happening onstage no matter what seat they're in. Performances are typically held on Thursday through Sunday during the run of a show. Tickets can be purchased online or in-person at the box office.

4039 NW 16th Blvd., 352-376-4949
gcplayhouse.org

OTHER LOCAL THEATERS TO CHECK OUT

Acrosstown Repertory Theatre
3501 SW 2nd Ave. Ste. O, 352-234-6278
acrosstown.org

High Springs Playhouse
23416 W US Hwy. 27, High Springs, 386-454-3525
highspringsplayhouse.com

39

WATCH A PERFORMANCE
AT THE PHILLIPS CENTER

Immerse yourself in the charm of live performance at one of Gainesville's most well-known venues, the Curtis M. Phillips Center for the Performing Arts. From Broadway productions to enchanting classical concerts, dance performances, and theater productions, the Phillips Center offers a huge range of productions that appeal to every taste and interest. You could catch a local comedy act one night and watch an internationally acclaimed orchestra the next. The Phillips Center features multiple performance spaces, including a main theater with seating for over 1,700 guests and smaller venues for more intimate performances and events. Performances are offered multiple times a week on varying dates and times. With world-class acoustics and high-quality amenities, attending a performance at the Phillips Center is the perfect way to spend an evening immersed in the arts.

3201 Hull Rd., 352-392-2787
performingarts.ufl.edu

40

SEE THE CURIOSITIES
AT THE THEATRE OF MEMORY

Step into the enchanting Theatre of Memory to discover a truly one-of-a-kind museum. It's a unique and eclectic collection of artifacts, memorabilia, documents, cultural objects from around the world, and so much more. The museum's founder and curator, Bill Hutchinson, has been personally collecting the objects for decades. He is a walking museum himself, sharing his knowledge and passion as he talks about the history of the pieces on display. One-of-a-kind treasures in the museum range from a dinosaur egg to a collection of historic teapots to a pair of John Lennon's glasses. Each item has an interesting story behind it, and Bill will gladly give you an interactive tour through the collection while telling the stories behind these unique pieces. The Theatre of Memory is free and open Wednesday through Sunday, 10:30 a.m. to 4:30 p.m.

1705 NW 6th St., 352-318-2633
theatreofmemory.org

BE INSPIRED
AT ARTWALK

On the last Friday of every month, artists and creatives put on a show in downtown Gainesville. This free, self-guided art experience allows you to visit over a dozen local venues, galleries, and eateries in downtown and the surrounding areas. You'll get the chance to see the community's abundance of creativity through art exhibitions, shows, and live performances at each stop. The event runs from 7 to 10 p.m., with some of the stops walkable within the downtown area. The venues vary from month to month, and each Artwalk will showcase different art and experiences. Some of the offerings include interactive art stations, live music, refreshments, and vendor markets. Artwalk is a celebration of the creativity in Gainesville and a great way to bring together the artists and the local community.

artwalkgainesville.com

CELEBRATE FOURTH OF JULY
THE SMALL-TOWN WAY

The small towns surrounding Gainesville offer festive and community-oriented Fourth of July celebrations that capture the spirit of Americana. In towns like High Springs, Alachua, and Micanopy, residents and visitors alike gather for family-friendly festivities and fireworks. Micanopy offers a fun Independence Day parade along Northeast Cholokka Boulevard during the day, and fireworks and celebrations in the evening. The city of Alachua hosts a big event, billed as the "Largest Small Town Fireworks Display in America." Enjoy food trucks, live music, kids' activities, and, of course, a fantastic fireworks show. Red, White & Boom takes place in Archer and features food vendors, games and activities, and a fireworks display. Don't forget to bring folding chairs or a picnic blanket to watch the fireworks. These small-town Fourth of July festivities offer a great opportunity for communities to come together and celebrate.

micanopytown.com
cityofalachua.com
cityofarcher.com

For a great chance to see big alligators up close, head to La Chua Trail.

SPORTS AND RECREATION

VISIT A CHAMPION
AT CELLON OAK PARK

Have you ever seen a champion tree? A champion tree is the largest tree of its species, either in circumference, height, or crown spread (or sometimes all three!). The former Florida champion live oak tree resides right here at Cellon Oak Park in Gainesville. The magnificent Cellon Oak, named after the previous landowner, stands as the focal point of the park. The tree has a circumference of 30 feet, a height of 85 feet, a crown spread of 160 feet, and is estimated to be over 200 years old. It was the Florida champion until October 2022, when it was dethroned by another live oak tree in a private residence in the town of Alachua. The sprawling, shady branches of the Cellon Oak are a perfect backdrop for a picnic, family photos, or a small wedding ceremony. The free park has picnic tables and grills, but no restrooms.

4100 NW 169th Pl., 352-264-6847
alachuacounty.us/depts/parks/pages/parkslist.aspx

ADMIRE PLANTS AND FLOWERS
AT KANAPAHA BOTANICAL GARDENS

A peaceful garden oasis is one of the last things you might expect to find in the middle of bustling southwest Archer Road. But that's exactly what Kanapaha Botanical Gardens is. This large botanical garden is home to hundreds of varieties of plants, from the largest herb garden in the Southeast to the largest public display of bamboo in Florida. The gardens are all viewable from an accessible 1.5-mile paved path. Multiple waterfalls, gazebos, and benches are spread throughout the gardens to allow visitors to stop and enjoy the tranquility. To keep the kids entertained, there's a children's garden, playground, and labyrinth hedge maze. In the summertime you can see the giant Victoria water lilies, which can grow up to 6 feet in diameter! Kanapaha Botanical Gardens costs $10 per adult and $5 per child ages 5 to 13. It is open daily year-round except major holidays, but a visit in June through September will yield the most color and flowers in bloom.

4700 SW 58th Dr., 352-372-4981
kanapaha.org

CLIMB DOWN INSIDE A SINKHOLE

AT DEVIL'S MILLHOPPER GEOLOGICAL STATE PARK

For a unique and adventurous activity, head to Devil's Millhopper Geological State Park where you can venture down inside a 120-foot-deep sinkhole! Inside the sinkhole is like a mini rainforest—lush, green plants grow all over the sides; birds and insects chirp; and small waterfalls trickle down to the bottom after a good rain. A 132-step staircase descends into the sinkhole and ends with a boardwalk viewing platform at the bottom. The amount of water at the bottom depends on the season and recent rainfall. This unique natural wonder has been drawing visitors since the 1880s, and the Civilian Conservation Corps reportedly built the first staircase to view the sinkhole in the 1930s. There are a couple of accessible lookout points from the paved pathway at the top, but the best views come from venturing down inside. Ranger-led tours are available each Saturday at 10 a.m.

4732 Millhopper Rd., 352-955-2008
floridastateparks.org

BIKE, WALK, OR SKATE

THE GAINESVILLE–HAWTHORNE STATE TRAIL

The Gainesville–Hawthorne State Trail runs for 16 miles, starting at Boulware Springs Nature Park in Gainesville and extending into the town of Hawthorne. Grab your bike, your roller skates, your dog, your horse, or a walking buddy, and get in some miles on the trail. The free trail is entirely paved, with a grassy horseback riding trail running alongside it. With multiple overlooks and parks to stop at along the way, the trail has plenty of sights to keep your interest. Check out Paynes Prairie, Alachua Lake, or the Prairie Creek Boardwalk. Along the way, you'll also see interpretive signs about the history of the railroad in Gainesville since the trail was once a historic railbed. To access the trail, there are a few trailheads with parking areas.

Boulware Springs Nature Park, 3300 SE 15th St.

Intersection of County Rds. 234 and 2082, Rochelle
(at Prairie Creek Preserve)

7902 SE 200th Dr., off County Rd. 2082, west of Hawthorne

2182 SE 71st Ave., Hawthorne

352-466-3397
floridastateparks.org

47

ROOT FOR THE FLORIDA GATORS
AT THE SWAMP

Nothing says Gainesville like cheering on the hometown Florida Gators at The Swamp. This thrilling experience embodies the spirit of college football and brings the whole town together each game day. The iconic Ben Hill Griffin Stadium, aka The Swamp, is located in the heart of the University of Florida campus. With a capacity of over 88,000 fans, the stadium is known for its intimidating atmosphere and loud crowds. The Swamp is not just a venue, it's a hallowed ground where orange-and-blue-clad fans gather and cheers of "Go Gators!" fill the air. Traditions such as the famous "Gator Chomp" or singing Tom Petty's "I Won't Back Down" at the end of the third quarter create an unforgettable experience of camaraderie. Rooting for the Florida Gators at The Swamp is not just about football, it's about being part of the community and the proud legacy of Gator Nation. Every Gainesville resident should experience it at least once!

157 Gale Lemerand Dr., 352-375-4683
floridagators.com

TIP

The University of Florida is home to a number of other sports teams in addition to football. Root for your team at a Gators baseball game at Condron Ballpark, or a men's basketball game at the Stephen C. O'Connell Center. Find your favorite Gators sport to watch!

Condron Ballpark
2800 Citrus Rd.
floridagators.com/sports/baseball

Stephen C. O'Connell Center
250 Gale Lemerand Dr.
floridagators.com/sports/mens-basketball

CHASE WATERFALLS
AT CEDAR LAKES WOODS & GARDENS

For an enchanting day spent admiring a beautiful botanical garden, head south to Cedar Lakes Woods & Gardens in Williston. The sunken lakes are the centerpiece of the garden, with meandering paths, cascading waterfalls, and blooming plants all around. The unique layout of Cedar Lakes Woods & Gardens stemmed from an abandoned limestone quarry, which was salvaged and transformed through the vision of Dr. Raymond Webber. Now, visitors can explore the 20 intertwined gardens, koi-filled ponds, gazebos, and multiple bridge-connected islands. When you're ready for a snack, there are many great spots for a picnic within the grounds. The cost is $12 per adult and $7 per child ages 6 to 13. During Christmastime, the gardens are transformed into a stunning display of lights and decorations for the Christmas in the Quarry event. It's a wonderfully festive sight to see!

4990 NE 180th Ave., Williston, 352-529-0055
cedarlakeswoodsandgarden.com

TIP

For a fun day trip, group this together with next door Devil's Den Spring for an epic underground snorkel. Once you've worked up an appetite, have a classic Southern meal at the historic Ivy House Restaurant!

Devil's Den Spring
5390 NE 180th Ave., Williston, 352-528-3344
devilsden.com

The Ivy House
106 NW Main St., Williston, 352-528-5410

49

LEARN ABOUT ANIMALS
AT SANTA FE COLLEGE TEACHING ZOO

Take a walk through the Santa Fe College Teaching Zoo to see over 70 species of monkeys, birds, reptiles, and small mammals up close. A quarter-mile accessible shaded path winds through the exhibits. This is a unique educational institution that blends hands-on learning with wildlife conservation. Located on the Santa Fe College campus, this teaching zoo serves as a living classroom where students in the Zoo Animal Technology program can gain practical experience in the care and management of animal species. Interactive exhibits, guided tours, and special events give the public a chance to view the animals while supporting educational initiatives. The paths at the zoo are wheelchair and stroller accessible, making this a perfect activity for the whole family. The zoo is open daily from 9 a.m. to 3 p.m., except on major holidays. It costs $10 per adult and $6 for children ages 4 to 12 and seniors age 60 and older. There are also discounts available for teachers, students, military, and first responders.

3000 NW 83rd St., 352-395-5633
sfcollege.edu/zoo

FOLLOW HOGTOWN CREEK
THROUGH GAINESVILLE

Hogtown Creek spans over 20 miles through Gainesville, from the headwaters to a sinkhole where it disappears underground. The tranquility of Hogtown Creek offers an escape from the neighborhoods and city streets just outside the park bounds. The creek and the surrounding forests and wetlands can be enjoyed from several nature parks, collectively known as the Hogtown Creek Greenway. Multiple trailheads provide miles of shady hiking and biking trails, boardwalks, picnic areas, and playgrounds. Hogtown Creek Headwaters Nature Park is home to a trail, playground, and a nature center with exhibits and information about the creek. Over a mile of trails with bluffs above the creek await at Alfred A. Ring Park. Loblolly Woods Nature Park has beautiful trails and towering namesake loblolly pines. Don't forget to check out the section of the park across Eighth Avenue where there's an accessible boardwalk. Parking is available at all three of these trailheads. Plus, they are free and dog friendly!

Hogtown Creek Headwaters Nature Park: 1500 NW 45th Ave.
Alfred A. Ring Park: 1801 NW 23rd Blvd.
Loblolly Woods Nature Park: 3315 NW 5th Ave.

352-334-5000
gainesvillefl.gov/parks

LOOK FOR ALLIGATORS
AT SWEETWATER WETLANDS PARK

For a breath of fresh air, take a walk through Sweetwater Wetlands Park and look for alligators, turtles, and birds. Covering over 125 acres, there are boardwalks and accessible paths through several different wetlands areas. The park primarily serves as a means to filter water going into Paynes Prairie, utilizing natural wetland processes to improve water quality. But it's also a haven for wildlife and a recreational retreat for visitors. Educational signs along the trails show the importance of wetland ecosystems and their role in sustaining biodiversity. The majority of the trails are in full sun, so be sure to bring water and sun protection. Sweetwater Wetlands Park is known as a birding hot spot in Gainesville. Each Wednesday morning, the Alachua Audubon Society offers a guided Bird Walk at the Wetlands at 8:30 a.m., September through May. Park admission is $5 per vehicle.

325 SW Williston Rd., 352-554-5871
gainesvillefl.gov/parks

TIP

For more nature time, head just down the road to the free Sweetwater Preserve. There are about three miles of trails here that wind by Sweetwater Branch, through floodplains, and in various ecosystems. And if you're hungry after all your hiking, stop at 43rd Street Deli, a beloved family owned spot for breakfast and lunch.

Sweetwater Preserve
309 SE 16th Ave., 352-264-6800
alachuacounty.us/depts/parks/pages/parkslist.aspx

43rd Street Deli (south location)
3483 SW Williston Rd., 352-373-5656
43rdstreetdeli.com

MEET EXOTIC ANIMALS
AT CARSON SPRINGS WILDLIFE CONSERVATION FOUNDATION

You might be surprised to find that tigers, leopards, and lions are living in Gainesville! Carson Springs Wildlife Conservation Foundation is a nonprofit organization dedicated to the rescue, rehabilitation, and conservation of exotic and endangered species. The foundation serves as a sanctuary for animals, including a number of big cats, primates, and birds, many of which have been rescued from abusive or neglectful situations. At Carson Springs, the animals are provided with spacious habitats filled with trees and bushes, allowing them to live in a natural and enriching environment. The foundation also focuses on education and outreach, offering educational programs to raise awareness about wildlife conservation and the importance of protecting endangered species. To visit the facility, book a spot on a zoologist-led walking tour, typically offered Saturdays at 10 a.m. Tickets cost $35 for adults and $15 for children ages 2 to 11. Private tours also can be booked, and open houses and other special events are offered throughout the year.

8528 E County Rd. 225, 352-468-2827
carsonspringswildlife.org

53

SEE THE AZALEAS
AT RAVINE GARDENS STATE PARK

Although it's a little bit farther outside Gainesville in Palatka, a visit to Ravine Gardens State Park is so worth the drive. A trip in late January through March will yield a beautiful, colorful bloom of azaleas all around the park. The park features a combination of historic formal gardens, challenging hiking trails, ravines, and small springs. Two historic suspension bridges provide a fun vantage point over the ravines. The Azalea Trail, considered strenuous, winds around the ravine and up and down stairs and hills. This is one of the best parks in the area for hiking with elevation changes! A paved trail wraps around the top of the ravine offering an accessible path for cycling and walking to see the flowers. As one of Florida's nine original New Deal–era state parks created in the 1930s, Ravine Gardens is full of history. The lush greenery and blooms, fun hiking trails, and beautiful spring-fed creek make Ravine Gardens well worth a visit!

1600 Twigg St., Palatka, 386-329-3721
floridastateparks.org

PLAY
AT DEPOT PARK

Depot Park is an urban park that offers a combination of green space, paved paths, family-friendly recreational facilities, and community events. Situated on the former site of the Gainesville Train Depot, the park now has a scenic setting with ponds and wetlands. The southern half of the park is designated as a nature preserve, where you can see wetlands with a variety of plants and wildlife. Depot Park's lawn areas are perfect for picnicking, playing sports, or simply relaxing and enjoying the outdoors. Depot Park features a state-of-the-art playground and splash pad, making it a favorite spot for families. Inside the depot building, you can grab a bite to eat or a cold beverage from Parkside Convenience Shop, Goldie's Burgers, or Boxcar Beer & Wine Garden. Throughout the year, Depot Park hosts a variety of community events, concerts, and festivals, ranging from outdoor movie nights to food truck rallies.

874 SE 4th St.
depotpark.org

TIP

Another great playground in Gainesville is at Albert "Ray" Massey Park, also known as Westside Park. This newly renovated playground is now space-themed, inspired by the adjacent Solar Walk on Eighth Avenue. This is Gainesville's first fully inclusive playground, meaning it's accessible to children of all ages and abilities.

1001 NW 34th St.
gainesvillefl.gov/parks

LOOK FOR ALLIGATORS, BISON, AND WILD HORSES
AT PAYNES PRAIRIE PRESERVE STATE PARK

Did you know there are herds of wild bison and horses in Florida? Visit Paynes Prairie Preserve State Park for a chance to see them, plus plenty of alligators and birds. Paynes Prairie covers nearly 23,000 acres of various ecosystems and rich biodiversity. Visitors can enjoy hiking, biking, and horseback riding on over 30 miles of trails throughout three trailheads. The main entrance offers one of the park's highlights—a 50-foot-tall observation tower that provides panoramic views of the prairie (bring your binoculars!). The La Chua Trail is home to a boardwalk and trail out into the prairie, where you're almost certain to see big gators on the water's edge. This is one of my favorite places to bring out-of-state guests to see our famous Florida alligators. The Bolen Bluff Trailhead is one of the best opportunities to see the bison, especially early or late in the day. Other activities in Paynes Prairie Preserve include fishing, paddling, and camping.

Main Entrance: 100 Savannah Blvd., Micanopy
La Chua Trailhead: 4801 Camp Ranch Rd.
Bolen Bluff Trailhead: Off US Hwy. 441, Micanopy

352-466-3397
floridastateparks.org

SNORKEL A PREHISTORIC UNDERGROUND SPRING AT DEVIL'S DEN

Devil's Den Spring is a natural spring inside a cave. A hole in the top of the cave lets in natural light and has vines cascading down, creating a stunning picturesque setting. Ancient rock formations and fossil beds line the walls of the cave, which descends over 50 feet down. Both snorkeling and scuba diving can be enjoyed in the spring, but general swimming is not permitted. For snorkelers, reservations are required, and be sure to make them early—weekend slots can and do sell out. Scuba divers do not need to make a reservation but do need an open water certification and a diving buddy. Equipment for both snorkeling and scuba diving can be rented from the dive center. Devil's Den is open seven days a week, except Christmas Day. Visiting this natural wonder is well worth it to experience the beauty of the underground and underwater world!

5390 NE 180th Ave., Williston, 352-528-3344
devilsden.com

TUBE A CRYSTAL-CLEAR RIVER AT ICHETUCKNEE SPRINGS STATE PARK

Tubing a spring-fed river is a quintessential Florida experience, and there's no better place than the crystal-clear Ichetucknee River. Ichetucknee Springs State Park is less than an hour north in Fort White. Visitors can rent tubes at the park and enjoy a tranquil float down the river surrounded by trees. The water is a cool 72 degrees year-round, making for a refreshing activity during the hot summer. You will spot fish, birds, and turtles during the journey, and if you're lucky, maybe even a river otter. All ages can enjoy tubing on the river, but little ones may prefer a tube with a mesh bottom. The tubing trip can take approximately 45–90 minutes, depending on which point you choose to launch from. After you've finished tubing, you can enjoy swimming and snorkeling in the headwaters of Ichetucknee Springs State Park. Tubing not your thing? You also can kayak, canoe, or paddleboard on the river.

12087 SW US 27 Hwy., Fort White, 386-497-1500
ichetuckneesprings.com

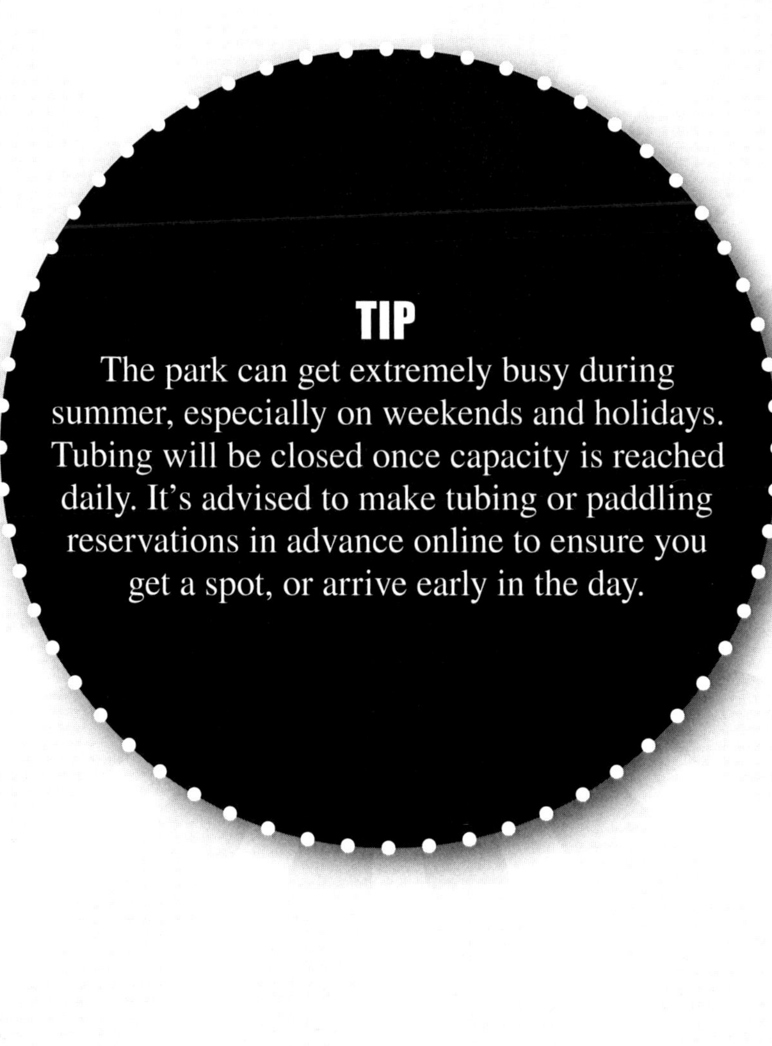

TIP

The park can get extremely busy during summer, especially on weekends and holidays. Tubing will be closed once capacity is reached daily. It's advised to make tubing or paddling reservations in advance online to ensure you get a spot, or arrive early in the day.

MOUNTAIN BIKE
AT SAN FELASCO HAMMOCK PRESERVE STATE PARK

If you're looking for a premier destination for mountain biking near Gainesville, look no further than San Felasco Hammock Preserve State Park. The park's north entrance in Alachua is well known as one of the best spots for off-road biking in the area. An extensive network of trails winds through diverse ecosystems with views of creeks, sinkholes, and ravines. With nearly 20 miles of trails, ranging in difficulty from beginner to advanced, San Felasco provides an exhilarating experience for riders of all levels. The landscape offers some challenging terrain, like natural obstacles and hills, making it an ideal spot for anyone seeking an adventurous mountain biking experience. There are also equestrian trails at the park's north entrance. Riders can explore the beauty of the park while navigating the winding trails and enjoying the forested surroundings. Hikers are welcome to use any of the trails at the north trailhead, or head to the park's south trailhead, where there are several hiking-only trails.

North Trailhead
13201 San Felasco Pkwy., Alachua
(biking, equestrian, and hiking)

South Trailhead
11101 Millhopper Rd. (hiking only)

352-955-2008
floridastateparks.org

TIP

For more challenging mountain bike trails, check out the Santos Trailhead in Ocala. Part of the Marjorie Harris Carr Cross Florida Greenway, this former limerock quarry provides exciting terrain for mountain bikers from beginners to experts. Santos has over 80 miles of trails and even has a campground so you can spend multiple days riding through everything it has to offer.

3080 SE 80th St., Ocala, 352-369-2693
floridastateparks.org

SEE A DUGOUT CANOE
AT NEWNANS LAKE STATE FOREST

Leave the hustle and bustle of the city and escape to Newnans Lake State Forest, a recreation area encompassing over 1,000 acres of land on the shores of Lake Newnan. Shady trails for hiking and mountain biking wind through forests and swamps at two trailheads: the Lake Pithlachocco Trailhead and the West Hiking Trailhead. Newnans Lake holds a fascinating world of history beneath its surface—over 100 Native American dugout canoes rest within the lake bed. In 2000, several years of drought exposed the canoes. They were all estimated to be between 500 and 5,000 years old, making the lake the single largest recorded site of ancient watercraft known in North America. A replica canoe and information are on display at Newnans Lake State Forest, at the end of the Lake Pithlachocco East Hiking Trail right by the lake. A day-use pass costs $2 per vehicle, and make sure to bring exact change.

5353 NE 39th Ave., 352-395-4932
fdacs.gov/forest-wildfire/our-forests/state-forests/newnans-lake-state-forest

SUPPORT A CAUSE
AT A 5K

There are a variety of 5K races throughout the year in Gainesville, many of which are dedicated to supporting local causes or nonprofit organizations. These events provide an opportunity for runners and walkers of all levels to make a positive impact on the community while staying active. The Hogtown 5K Beer Run, presented by Swamp Head Brewery, benefits the Climb for Cancer Foundation to support cancer patients being treated at UF Health. The Florida Springs Run and Spring Fest supports the Florida Springs Institute with a day of festivities at First Magnitude Brewing Company. If you're an animal lover, lace up your running shoes on Thanksgiving Day for the Turkey Trot at Critter Creek Farm Sanctuary. The Guano Run, hosted by Blackadder Brewing Company, supports the Lubee Bat Conservancy's mission of bat conservation and education. With scenic routes, great causes, and a supportive atmosphere, Gainesville's 5K races offer a rewarding experience that combines fitness, philanthropy, and community spirit.

climbforcancerfoundation.org
floridaspringsinstitute.org
crittercreekfarmsanctuary.org
lubee.org/guanorun

61

RIDE A WORLD-FAMOUS GLASS BOTTOM BOAT
AT SILVER SPRINGS STATE PARK

Silver Springs State Park is home to the oldest attraction in Florida: the glass bottom boats. Step aboard your boat and prepare to be mesmerized as you glide over the beautiful Silver River and look at the underwater world through the transparent floor. Passengers can see multiple spring vents, submerged artifacts, fish, turtles, and more. Knowledgeable guides share information on the park's history, ecology, and wildlife, making the experience both educational and entertaining. You'll see a Native American dugout canoe, ancient trees, and even submerged statues. The crystal-clear water and jungle-like landscape make for a beautiful trip. Thirty-minute tours are offered every 15 to 20 minutes, 365 days a year. Online reservations are encouraged, especially on weekends. There's also an extended 90-minute tour offered Fridays through Mondays. In addition to the boat tour, Silver Springs State Park has many more activities to enjoy. Hiking trails, biking, kayaking, camping, a history museum, and picnicking are some of the other things to do here.

5656 E Silver Springs Blvd., Silver Springs, 352-261-5840
floridastateparks.org/silversprings

TEST YOUR BRAVERY
AT CANYONS ZIP LINE AND ADVENTURE PARK

Cliffs don't usually come to mind when thinking about North Central Florida, but head 45 minutes south to Ocala, and you'll see where the Canyons Zip Line and Adventure Park gets its name. With the longest, highest, and fastest zip lines in Florida, this exhilarating adventure is not for the faint of heart. Created around an old limestone quarry, the Canyons is home to multiple zip lines of varying lengths and heights. With breathtaking views of forests, blue lakes, and incredible limestone canyons, the zip line courses are truly thrilling. The park also offers horseback riding tours and kayaking tours for those who prefer to stay closer to the ground while still having an adventurous outdoor experience. The zip lines are suitable for participants of any skill level age 10 or older, making this a great activity for families, friends, and groups looking for an adventure. Head to the website to check available dates and times and to make your reservation.

8045 NW Gainesville Rd. (CR 25A), Ocala, 352-351-9477
zipthecanyons.com

GO GLAMPING
AT MOONSHINE ACRES

Love spending time outdoors, but camping's not your thing? Try the luxurious glamping experience at Moonshine Acres. Nestled in the forests near Fort White, this hidden gem offers a blend of rustic charm and modern comfort. With RV sites and 10 glamping tents, this park allows you to unwind and enjoy nature without sacrificing convenience. Perfect for family adventures, the glamping tents sleep up to four people and some even come with bunk beds. They include a mini fridge and air conditioning. On-site amenities include a playground, clubhouse and game room, firepits, a general store, and a dog park. Moonshine Acres is only a few miles from Ichetucknee Springs State Park, where you can enjoy tubing, swimming, or paddling. The Santa Fe River is less than a 10-minute drive, along with several other parks and preserves to explore. This area is made up of small towns, so there are plenty of antique shops and local restaurants to try nearby.

10089 US Hwy. 27, Fort White, 833-744-6378
moonshineacresrvpark.com

PADDLE THE SPRINGS
ON THE SANTA FE RIVER

Hop in a canoe or kayak and embark on a scenic journey down the Santa Fe River. A great place to start your paddle is Gilchrist Blue Springs State Park, where you can launch your own vessel or rent one at the park. A trip down the Santa Fe provides opportunities to see wildlife, beautiful scenery, and many natural springs. You'll know you've found a spring when you see the dark tannic river water mingle with blue spring water. You can paddle into these springs and enjoy a refreshing dip in the water while you visit. For a full day of adventure on the river, pack a picnic lunch and plenty of water. If you'd prefer to have a guide show you the best spots on the river, there are several tour companies in the area. Most offer rentals and shuttle services as well.

Gilchrist Blue Springs State Park
7450 NE 60th St., High Springs, 386-454-1369
floridastateparks.org

65

EXPLORE THE TRAILS
AT BLUES CREEK RAVINE PRESERVE

Blues Creek Ravine Preserve, located in northwest Gainesville, is a nearly untouched nature preserve protecting Blues Creek and an extensive ravine system. The preserve encompasses two trails for hiking or biking, totaling about 1.5 miles. The trails wind through the hilly landscape and provide elevated views of the creek plus opportunities for birding and wildlife sightings. The trails even offer some elevation changes. The preserve is a wonderful example of an undeveloped upland hardwood hammock forest, and there are no facilities or amenities here. Sinkholes, wetlands, and a bridge over the creek make hiking here a unique and fun experience. The Alachua Conservation Trust manages this preserve, and they offer weekly Walk and Talks on Friday afternoons, sometimes at Blues Creek Ravine Preserve. More information about events can be found on the website.

6710 NW 69th Ave., 352-373-1078
alachuaconservationtrust.org/blues-creek-ravine-preserve-guide

The parking area for Blues Creek Ravine Preserve is not right at the trailhead, but just a short walk away on the shoulder of Northwest 71st Street. Once you park, the trailhead is down Northwest 69th Avenue, which is a dirt road. Alternatively, you can bike to the trailhead.

FEED THE RETIRED HORSES
AT MILL CREEK FARM

The Retirement Home for Horses at Mill Creek Farm is a haven for retired horses in Alachua and a treat for any animal lover. This nonprofit organization provides a loving and safe environment for elderly horses who have been rescued from neglectful or abusive situations. The horses now enjoy spacious pastures, specialized care, and plenty of attention. They get to live out their retirement peacefully in this sanctuary without ever being worked or ridden again. Visitors are welcome to tour the farm and meet the horses on Saturdays from 11 a.m. to 3 p.m. Admission costs two carrots, but you'll probably want to bring extra to feed the horses. Kids and adults alike will love petting and feeding the more than 130 horses. Paths at the farm are paved, but there can be a lot of walking to get around the extensive grounds.

20307 NW CR 235A, Alachua, 386-462-1001
millcreekfarm.org

GO SCALLOPING
IN STEINHATCHEE

Escape to the gulf waters of Steinhatchee for a day of adventure spent scalloping. With its abundant scallop beds and relatively long scalloping season, Steinhatchee is one of the most popular places for this activity. If you don't have a boat, you can book a charter boat and guide to take you out on the water. Float on the surface in shallow water and search the seabed for these treasures, diving down to collect the ones you spot. No diving experience is required, although it helps to be a good swimmer and comfortable with a snorkel. After your successful day of scalloping, head back to shore to savor your fresh catch. Kathi's Krab Shack is a local favorite that can cook your scallops to your liking, and they also offer an abundance of other seafood dishes on the menu. Scallop season is open from June until September each year in the Steinhatchee area, making this the perfect summertime activity.

Kathi's Krab Shack
202 15th St. E, Steinhatchee, 352-498-0605
kathiskrabs.com

steinhatchee.com/scalloping-information

68

HIKE
THE FLORIDA NATIONAL SCENIC TRAIL

Have you ever thought about hiking the Appalachian Trail? Did you know that Florida has its own national scenic trail? The Florida Trail spans approximately 1,500 miles from south Florida to the panhandle, winding through some of the state's most beautiful landscapes. Whether you're ready to try overnight backpacking or just want to get some miles in, this is the perfect place. There are a ton of designated trailheads, but one of the coolest is the Landbridge Trailhead. Here you can hike about 1.2 miles out to the bridge that crosses right over Interstate 75. The goal of creating this more natural bridge was to offer a safe way to cross the interstate for pedestrians and wildlife. The trailhead even offers dedicated trails for hiking, cycling, and horseback riding. The Florida Trail is accessible to hikers of all skill levels.

11100 SW 16th Ave., Ocala, 850-523-8500
fs.usda.gov/fnst

OTHER NEARBY TRAILHEADS

Mike Roess Gold Head Branch State Park
Inside the entrance near the ranger station
6239 State Rd. 21, Keystone Heights

Fieldhouse Trailhead at Etoniah Creek State Forest
390 Holloway Rd., Florahome

Marshall Swamp Trailhead
at Marjorie Harris Carr Cross Florida Greenway
8282 SE Hwy. 314, Ocala

69

DISCOVER OLD FLORIDA
AT RAINBOW SPRINGS STATE PARK

Step into the enchanting beauty of Rainbow Springs State Park, a hidden gem less than an hour away in Dunnellon. This park was once an Old Florida roadside attraction, drawing people from all over the country to see the stunning springs and jungle-like surroundings. Today, you can stroll along the paved trails and enjoy the tranquil ambiance of the park's gardens and natural springs. Marvel at the three lush, human-made waterfalls cascading from rocks above. You might be surprised to see waterfalls this tall in Florida! Or dip your toes into the refreshing waters of Rainbow Springs and enjoy a picnic under the shade of ancient oak trees. For a longer day on the water, you can rent kayaks to paddle down the Rainbow River, or take a tube and gently float down. Whether you're seeking a peaceful retreat in nature or a fun-filled day on the water, a visit to Rainbow Springs State Park is well worth the trip.

19158 SW 81st Place Rd., Dunnellon, 352-465-8555
floridastateparks.org

SEE A DISAPPEARING RIVER
AT O'LENO STATE PARK

Did you know the Santa Fe River disappears underground at O'Leno State Park and rises again about three miles away? The river flows into a sinkhole, where it goes deep underground, and then reemerges at River Rise Preserve. O'Leno State Park encompasses over 6,000 acres of hardwood hammock, sinkholes, and swamps, plus over 11 miles of multiuse trails. It sits on the site of the historic town of Leno, which was founded in the 1800s. The Civilian Conservation Corps played a big role in constructing many of the buildings and structures here, including a suspension bridge crossing the Santa Fe River. Recreational activities range from hiking and birding along scenic trails to fishing, swimming, and kayaking on the river. A campground allows visitors to stay overnight to fully immerse themselves in the natural surroundings. To see where the river rises again, head over to River Rise Preserve, either via hiking a four-mile connector trail or driving to the trailhead.

O'Leno State Park
410 SE O'Leno Park Rd., High Springs, 386-454-1853
floridastateparks.org

River Rise Preserve
373 US Hwy. 27, High Springs

Tour the historic farmhouse
at Dudley Farm Historic State Park.

CULTURE AND HISTORY

71

SEE WHERE IT ALL STARTED
AT BOULWARE SPRINGS NATURE PARK

Boulware Springs holds a significant place in Gainesville's history. This spring was at one time the primary source of drinking water for the city. In 1854, Alachua County residents gathered for a picnic in the Boulware Springs area. It was here that they voted to move the county seat from Newnansville to a brand-new city, to be named Gainesville, to take advantage of the railway. This free water supply was one of the major factors that lured the University of Florida to settle in Gainesville rather than the planned Lake City. Today, the waterworks building stands in the center of Boulware Springs Nature Park. Although the building has fallen into disrepair over the years, the city of Gainesville is working toward a $2 million restoration project. At the park, enjoy views of the spring, picnic tables, and green space to play. This park also serves as a trailhead on the Gainesville–Hawthorne State Trail.

3300 SE 15th St., 352-334-5067
gainesvillefl.gov/parks

72

TOUR A FAMOUS AUTHOR'S HOME
AT MARJORIE KINNAN RAWLINGS HISTORIC STATE PARK

Have you ever read *The Yearling*? This famous work was written by Pulitzer Prize–winning author Marjorie Kinnan Rawlings, who once lived in a rural home just outside of Gainesville. Several of her writings were deeply inspired by her homestead in Cross Creek and the woods surrounding her home. Start your visit by walking through the gate Rawlings describes in her 1942 work *Cross Creek*: "step inside the rusty gate and close it behind . . . One is now inside the orange grove, out of one world and in the mysterious heart of another." At the park you can take a guided tour of the inside of her home, or take a self-guided tour of the grounds and explore her gardens and orange tree grove. Guided tours are given Thursday through Sunday at 10 a.m., 11 a.m., 1 p.m., 2 p.m., and 3 p.m. Directly adjacent to the park, there are picnic tables and a boat launch onto Orange Lake.

18700 S County Rd. 325, Cross Creek, 352-466-3672
floridastateparks.org

73

CHECK IN
TO THE HISTORIC SWEETWATER BRANCH INN

Historic elegance and Southern hospitality await when you check into the Sweetwater Branch Inn, a charming bed and breakfast in Gainesville's historic district. This enchanting Victorian inn offers an opportunity to step back in time and experience the charm of years gone by. With its beautifully restored rooms, lush gardens, and many amenities, Sweetwater Branch Inn is a special option for out-of-town guests, a romantic staycation, or just a peaceful retreat. A variety of uniquely decorated accommodations are available from guest suites to private cottages. Wake up to a delectable homemade breakfast, enjoy a leisurely stroll around the grounds, or simply relax on the porch with a glass of wine and a good book. Sweetwater Branch Inn is also a beloved wedding and events venue. With its warm atmosphere and timeless character, any stay at the historic Sweetwater Branch Inn surely will be memorable.

625 E University Ave., 352-373-6760
sweetwaterinn.com

74

IMMERSE YOURSELF IN LIVING HISTORY

AT MORNINGSIDE NATURE CENTER

For a dose of both nature and history, Morningside Nature Center is a great place to visit. Along with six miles of trails, picnic areas, and a playground, this park also has a mid-1800s Florida Living History Farm. Look through historic buildings like a Florida Cracker–style cabin built around 1840 and a one-room schoolhouse. On the first Saturday of each month from September through May, you can experience life on the farm as interpreters give hands-on demonstrations, do chores, and portray the daily life of a 19th-century homesteader. Kids and adults will love seeing heritage breed farm animals such as sheep, chickens, and even a cow. Each Wednesday, the Barnyard Buddies program offers a chance for visitors to meet and feed the animals. Morningside Nature Center also has a replica Timucuan village and a nature center with amphibian and reptile exhibits.

3540 E University Ave., 352-393-8240
gainesvillefl.gov/parks

TIP

For a bite to eat after visiting Morningside Nature Center, visit East End Eatery, just a few minutes down the road. This artsy and inviting spot serves breakfast and lunch with new specials daily. The cozy decor, a selection of books and board games to borrow, and a whole dedicated kids area make this restaurant feel like home!

1202 NE 8th Ave., 352-378-9870
eastendeatery.weebly.com

75

LEARN ABOUT FLORIDA'S HISTORY
AT THE FLORIDA MUSEUM OF NATURAL HISTORY

The Florida Museum of Natural History is one of the most widely visited attractions in Gainesville, and for good reason. This free museum on the University of Florida campus is one of the top five natural history museums in the country! Open year-round except major holidays, the museum is the perfect escape on a hot or rainy day. There are a bunch of engaging exhibits showcasing Florida's history and nature, like giant megalodon fossils, a palm-thatched Calusa leader's house, a full-scale coastal mangrove forest, and more. One of the most exciting exhibits is the Butterfly Rainforest, where you can walk through the lush, tropical garden and observe hundreds of free-flying butterflies plus waterfalls, fish, and birds. The Butterfly Rainforest costs $14 per adult or $7.50 per child ages 3 to 17. While you're here, head to the Harn Museum of Art right next door!

3215 Hull Rd., 352-846-2000
floridamuseum.ufl.edu

ADMIRE ARTWORK
AT THE HARN MUSEUM OF ART

Right next door to the Florida Museum of Natural History you'll find another wonderful free museum, the Harn Museum of Art. This is the perfect zen space for art and culture lovers in the center of Gainesville on the University of Florida campus. The museum displays paintings, photography, sculpture, and more from around the world in multiple rotating galleries. Even the building itself is a work of art with interesting architecture, gardens, and natural elements all around. Don't miss the *Florida Impressions: Gift of Samuel H. and Roberta T. Vickers* exhibit, an extensive collection of Florida-focused paintings showcasing the state's scenery, landmarks, and history. Free docent-led tours of the museum are offered every third Saturday of the month from 2 to 3 p.m. The Harn Museum is closed on Mondays and major holidays.

3259 Hull Rd., 352-392-9826
harn.ufl.edu

EXPERIENCE COASTAL OLD FLORIDA

IN CEDAR KEY

Head west to the Gulf Coast for a slice of Old Florida charm in Cedar Key. This cozy coastal town offers waterfront shopping and dining, sightseeing boat tours, and opportunities for fishing. Look for funky murals and art around the walkable downtown, or dolphins and shorebirds from the pier. At Cedar Key Museum State Park, learn about the history of the area, visit a restored 1800s home, or take a walk or paddle through the salt marshes. Stop in Cedar Keyhole Artists Co-op & Gallery to shop for locally made treasures. For an adventurous day trip, rent kayaks and paddle out to an island ghost town, Atsena Otie Key, which was the original location of the town. When you've worked up an appetite, taste the three-time World Champion Clam Chowder at Tony's Restaurant. If you prefer to make this a weekend getaway, there are several historic bed and breakfasts in Cedar Key. Cedar Key Bed & Breakfast is a great option.

Cedar Key Museum State Park
12231 SW 166th Ct., Cedar Key, 352-543-5350
floridastateparks.org

Cedar Keyhole Artists Co-op & Gallery
457 2nd St., Cedar Key, 352-543-5801

Tony's Restaurant
597 2nd St., Cedar Key, 352-543-0022
tonyschowder.com

Cedar Key Bed & Breakfast
810 3rd St., Cedar Key, 352-543-9000
cedarkeybedandbreakfast.com

78

WALK THE HISTORIC HIGHLIGHTS

ON THE UNIVERSITY OF FLORIDA CAMPUS

Walking around the historic University of Florida campus provides a glimpse into the university's rich history. Many of the historic buildings on campus were constructed in the early 1900s, and quite a few are now on the National Register of Historic Places. The old oak trees and beautifully landscaped plazas add a special touch to the brick buildings and walkways. One of the most iconic landmarks on campus is the 157-foot-tall Century Tower. A programmed chime rings every 15 minutes, and you might even catch a live carillon bell performance by UF carillonneurs. Plaza of the Americas is a central green space, surrounded by historic buildings, and is the perfect place for studying, gathering, and special events. Sledd Hall is one of the most photographed buildings on campus because of its iconic archway carved with intricate details and its picturesque courtyard. Wherever you wander on campus, you're sure to uncover some interesting history and beautiful sights!

Century Tower: 375 Newell Dr.
Plaza of the Americas: 1552 Union Rd.
Sledd Hall: 191 Fletcher Dr.

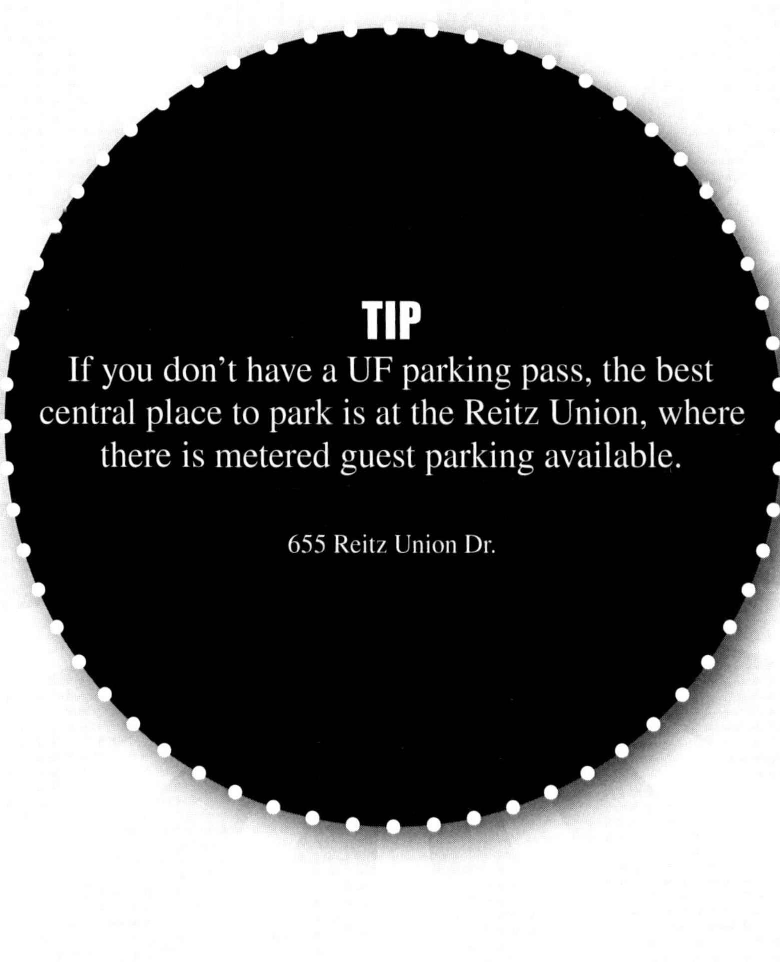
TIP
If you don't have a UF parking pass, the best central place to park is at the Reitz Union, where there is metered guest parking available.
655 Reitz Union Dr.

79

LEAVE A DRAWING
ON THE 34TH STREET WALL

The 34th Street Wall is a vibrant and iconic Gainesville landmark known for its ever-changing display of colorful graffiti and murals. Originally built in 1979 as a retaining wall, it has evolved over the years into something like a quirky community bulletin board. Spanning nearly a quarter of a mile long, the wall serves as a giant canvas for residents, students, and visitors to share messages and showcase their spray paint skills. The constantly changing artwork reflects the diverse perspectives and voices of the Gainesville community, covering a wide range of topics from pop culture and politics to personal reflections. Two panels on the wall are permanent memorials: one for the five victims of the Danny Rolling murders in 1990 and one honoring the late Tom Petty, a Gainesville native. Anything goes on the remaining sections of the wall, where new art is painted frequently, even daily. 34th Street is a busy road in Gainesville, so be mindful of traffic when you visit and stick to the sidewalk.

SW 34th St., between SW 2nd Ave. and Radio Rd.

VISIT
THE HISTORIC THOMAS CENTER

The Historic Thomas Center is a beautiful landmark that was built in 1910 as a residence for businessman and former Gainesville mayor William Reuben Thomas and his family. In 1928 it was renovated into the 94-room Thomas Hotel, hosting prominent guests such as Helen Keller and Robert Frost. In the 1970s it was purchased by the City of Gainesville and restored and repurposed into a multifaceted cultural center. Today, the Historic Thomas Center houses two art galleries, performance spaces, and event venues, hosting an array of concerts, lectures, and theatrical productions throughout the year. Visitors can explore the historic building and rotating art exhibits, or simply wander through the landscaped grounds and gardens. Virtual and audio tours of the Thomas Center are available online. Don't miss the Christmas lights, decorations, and tree lighting at the Thomas Center in December. The Thomas Center building's regular hours are Monday through Friday from 8 a.m. to 5 p.m. The galleries are open during regular hours, plus Saturdays from 1 to 4 p.m.

302 NE 6th Ave., 352-393-8539
historicthomascenter.org

81

UNLEASH YOUR INNER INVENTOR

AT THE CADE MUSEUM FOR CREATIVITY AND INVENTION

Step into a world where creativity and imagination have no bounds at the Cade Museum for Creativity and Invention. The museum is full of interactive exhibits that showcase the wonders of science, technology, engineering, art, and mathematics (STEAM), suitable for visitors of all ages. Explore the journey of invention through the eyes of pioneers like Dr. James Robert Cade, the lead inventor of Gatorade, and learn the stories behind some of the world's most groundbreaking discoveries. With rotating exhibits covering a wide range of topics and disciplines, the Cade Museum will have something new to discover on every visit. The museum also offers hands-on workshops and educational programs to inspire young minds and ignite a passion for learning. The Cade Museum is open Thursday through Sunday, 10 a.m. to 4 p.m. Admission costs $15 for adults and $10 for children ages 5 to 17. Located in Depot Park, there's plenty to do around the museum like enjoy the playground and restaurants.

811 S Main St., 352-371-8001
cademuseum.org

STEP BACK IN TIME
AT DUDLEY FARM HISTORIC STATE PARK

One of the unique state parks in Gainesville is Dudley Farm Historic State Park. In the 19th and 20th centuries, the Dudley family lived and established a farmstead here in what is now the area between Jonesville and Newberry. Today, you can explore the grounds and the 18 historic buildings, including the farmhouse with original furnishings, general store, and cane syrup complex. The park is open Wednesday through Sunday, 9 a.m. to 5 p.m. with the farmstead closing at 4 p.m. This historic farmstead is unique because all the buildings are original and have not been recreated or relocated. Dudley Farm is still a working farm with crops and livestock maintained by volunteers who are oftentimes dressed in period clothing. One of the best times of year to visit is during the annual Cane Grinding Festival, which occurs each November, where vendors sell goods and demonstrations highlight how life would have been on the farm.

18730 W Newberry Rd., Newberry, 352-472-1142
floridastateparks.org

TIP

Don't miss the Visitors Center right by the parking area when you first enter the park. The 12-minute film and interpretive displays really help to paint a picture of the three generations of the Dudley family before you walk over to the farmstead. Don't forget to grab a map for the self-guided walking tour.

83

CELEBRATE ART
AT THE ANNUAL DOWNTOWN FESTIVAL & ART SHOW

Don't miss the vibrant atmosphere and creative energy of the Downtown Festival & Art Show, held annually each November. This weekend-long event showcases the talents of local and traveling artists, offering a diverse range of art mediums, including painting, woodworking, photography, jewelry, and more. Running for over 40 years and now featuring more than 200 vendors, this is one of the largest art festivals in North Florida. Stroll through the historic streets of downtown Gainesville and explore rows and rows of booths. While you admire the art, stop into any of the local businesses downtown for a bite to eat or discover a new favorite shop. In addition to the art, the festival also features live music and entertainment performances, food vendors, and interactive activities for all ages.

gainesvilledowntownartfest.net

TIP

For easy parking downtown, try the Southwest Downtown Parking Garage. It's close to many locations and is at the western boundary of the festival. It has reasonable rates, so it's a great place to park all day. Plus, the garage is decorated with murals on almost every wall!

105 SW 3rd St.

EXPLORE GAINESVILLE'S PAST

AT THE MATHESON HISTORY MUSEUM

The Matheson History Museum gives a glimpse into Alachua County's history through exhibits, artifacts, and educational programs. Housed in a historic 1932 building, the museum's exhibits span a range of topics and time periods, from Native American history to the growth of Gainesville as a hub of education and culture. A large space for rotating exhibits ensures you can learn about something new every time you visit. In addition to the main exhibits, the historic 1867 Matheson House is also available to view by booking a guided tour. It is one of the three oldest residences in Gainesville, and you can see the rooms set up with period furniture and Matheson family belongings. The museum also hosts special events, classes, lectures, and workshops. A research library and archives are accessible to scholars, students, and members of the public interested in conducting historical research. Matheson History Museum is open Wednesday through Saturday from 11 a.m. to 4 p.m., and admission is free.

513 E University Ave., 352-378-2280
mathesonmuseum.org

85

SEE THE WRITING ON THE WALL AT HISTORIC HAILE HOMESTEAD

The Historic Haile Homestead, built in 1856, stands as one of the oldest and most well-preserved homes in North Central Florida. At this historic location, you can tour the Haile family's home and learn more about life on the plantation in the visitors center. The most unique and mysterious feature of the home is the "Talking Walls." For an unknown reason, the Haile family wrote all over the walls in the home. Everything from household inventory lists to children's growth charts to inscriptions by visitors are documented on the walls. Guided tours showcase how the Haile family lived on the Kanapaha Plantation and highlight the experiences of the enslaved people who lived and worked there. The Historic Haile Homestead is open to the public for guided tours on Saturdays from 10 a.m. to 2 p.m. and Sundays from noon to 4 p.m. Tours cost $5 per person or are free for children under 12 years old. Private tours can be scheduled throughout the week for $10 per person.

8500 SW Archer Rd., 352-336-9096
hailehomestead.org

TIP

Although the Historic Haile Homestead is all the way on the far west side of town, there are some dining options worth checking out in Haile Plantation if you're hungry. For fantastic coffee, ice cream, or pastries, head to Patticakes in the Village Monday through Saturday. And for American classics, cocktails, and great happy hour specials, try That Bar & Table, open daily for lunch and dinner.

Patticakes in the Village
9124 SW 51st Rd., Ste. B-102, 352-328-3945
patticakesgnv.com/patticakes-in-the-village

That Bar & Table
2725 SW 91st St., Ste. 100, 352-331-6620
thatbarandtable.com

There are so many antiques
to be found in Micanopy.

SHOPPING AND FASHION

HUNT FOR ANTIQUE TREASURES
IN MICANOPY

If you're looking for antique treasures, local art, and Old Florida charm, look no further than Micanopy. Founded in 1821 and believed to be the oldest inland town in Florida, Micanopy has no shortage of history. Start your day with a coffee and pastry from Mosswood Bakehouse, then walk down Cholokka Boulevard and admire the historic buildings surrounded by old oak trees dripping with Spanish moss. There are tons of little shops along this street to window shop or search for unique finds. If you like old headstones, don't miss the Micanopy Historic Cemetery, which dates back to 1826. You can spend hours browsing through the Antique City Mall—a great way to escape a hot afternoon or rain shower. Before you go, bring your appetite to the unassuming but delicious Pearl Country Store & Barbecue for a huge plate of barbecue. For one of the largest art festivals in the area, visit the Micanopy Fall Festival, held each October.

TIP

If you're looking to spend more time in Micanopy, stay at the historic Herlong Mansion Bed & Breakfast. It's right in the heart of the action in the historic downtown.

402 NE Cholokka Blvd., Micanopy, 352-466-3322
herlong.com

Mosswood Bakehouse
703 NE Cholokka Blvd., Micanopy, 352-466-5002
mosswoodbakehouse.com

Micanopy Historic Cemetery
401 W Smith Ave., Micanopy

Antique City Mall
17020 SE County Rd. 234, Micanopy, 352-389-4688
antiquecitymall.com

Pearl Country Store & Barbecue
106A NE Hwy. 441, Micanopy, 352-466-4025
pearlcountrystore.com

SCORE SECONDHAND FINDS AT THE REPURPOSE PROJECT

The Repurpose Project is so much more than just a thrift store. It's a unique initiative that focuses on saving reusable materials from becoming waste in landfills. This creative nonprofit promotes sustainability and environmental consciousness by providing a space for the community to donate, purchase, and repurpose items that might otherwise be thrown away. The Repurpose Project operates like a thrift store, but specifically emphasizes salvaging and reusing materials. By design, they accept junk—things that you wouldn't always find in a typical thrift store, but that you might find in the back of your grandparents' garage: scrap wood, fixtures, art supplies, fabric scraps, glassware, and so much more. The project not only provides affordable and unique finds for shoppers but also offers zero-waste education, community events, and classes, all promoting a more sustainable way of living in Gainesville. They also have a second store, Reuse Planet, which focuses on secondhand furnishings and appliances.

Repurpose Project
1920 NE 23rd Ave., 352-363-8902
repurposeproject.org

Reuse Planet
1540 NE Waldo Rd., 352-647-5112
reuseplanet.org

88

GROW YOUR GREEN THUMB
AT PLANTSTAY

Discover the ultimate destination for houseplant enthusiasts at Plantstay. Step into the inviting shop and be greeted by lush foliage and a tranquil jungle atmosphere. Plantstay offers a diverse selection of houseplants, succulents, and rare plants, with something for every plant lover, whether you're a novice plant parent or an experienced collector. From easy-care basics to statement-making foliage, each plant at Plantstay is hand-selected and carefully curated. The knowledgeable staff are passionate about plants and are always on hand to offer advice, tips, and recommendations to help you find the perfect plants for your space and lifestyle. Plantstay also offers frequent workshops like the popular "Recovering Plant Murderer" workshop to help turn brown thumbs green. Beyond the extensive plant collection, Plantstay also offers a variety of plant care essentials like pots and soil blends, plus plant-themed gifts and local goods.

3739 W University Ave., 352-400-4757
plantstay.com

89

FIND FRESH PRODUCE

AT THE HAILE VILLAGE FARMERS MARKET

Gainesville and the surrounding towns are home to multiple community farmers markets. With a market almost every day of the week from Archer to High Springs, there are plenty of opportunities to pick up locally grown produce, baked treats, farm-fresh eggs, plants, artisanal goods, and so much more. The Haile Village Farmers Market is one of the largest, where visitors can enjoy the vibrant booths filled with fresh produce, food vendors, live music, and a great community experience. The market offers more than just the typical produce—you also can grab fresh seafood and meat, homemade sauces and condiments, flowers and honey, and even goods such as candles and skin care. The Haile Village Farmers Market is a great place to support local growers and makers and connect with members of the community while enjoying the freshest ingredients and some of the most unique products Gainesville has to offer.

Saturdays 8:30 a.m.–noon
5213 SW 91 Ter.
hailefarmersmarket.com

OTHER FARMERS MARKETS IN THE AREA

Grove Street Farmers Market
Mondays 4–7 p.m.
Cypress and Grove Brewing Company, 1001 NW 4th St.

Archer Farmers Market
Tuesdays 3–7 p.m.
16994 SW 134th Ave., Archer

Union Street Farmers Market
Wednesdays 4–7 p.m.
Bo Diddley Plaza, 111 E University Ave.

GNV Farmers Market
Thursdays 4–7 p.m.
Heartwood Soundstage, 619 S Main St.

High Springs Farmers Market
Fridays 3–7 p.m.
23517 NW 185th Rd., High Springs

Alachua County Farmers Market
Saturdays 8:30 a.m.–noon
5920 NW 13th St.

90

BROWSE LOCAL ART
AT ARTISANS' GUILD GALLERY

Artisans' Guild Gallery showcases local artistic talent, providing a welcoming space for both artists and art enthusiasts alike. Established in 1970, this storied cooperative is one of the oldest in the country. The guild's mission for over five decades has been to provide a network and market for local artists. Located in a charming historic home in downtown Gainesville, the gallery features a diverse collection of handmade works for sale such as paintings, sculptures, ceramics, jewelry, and more. As a cooperative, Artisans' Guild Gallery fosters a sense of community among its members and patrons, creating a unique space for the appreciation and purchase of locally crafted art. Since it's staffed by the artists whose work is displayed, you're sure to have an inspiring conversation when you drop by. Whether you're looking to take home new treasures for yourself or find a thoughtful gift for a loved one, Artisans' Guild Gallery is a delightful place to shop. The gallery is open daily from 11 a.m. to 6 p.m.

224 NW 2nd Ave., 352-378-1383
artisansguildgallery.com

91

FIND AFFORDABLE FASHION AT SANDY'S BOUTIQUE

Sandy's Savvy Chic Resale Boutique is a stylish consignment shop offering a curated selection of gently used clothing, accessories, shoes, and home decor items. Sandy's gives shoppers the opportunity to find unique and fashionable pieces at a fraction of retail prices. The boutique's inventory includes a wide range of clothing, from casual everyday wear to designer labels. Customers can browse racks and racks filled with clothing for men and women, as well as shoes, designer handbags, jewelry, and accessories. Sandy's also features a selection of home items, including furniture and decor. Because it's a consignment boutique, you can also sell your gently used goods to Sandy's for extra cash. With its emphasis on quality, affordability, and sustainability, Sandy's Savvy Chic Resale Boutique is the perfect place for savvy shoppers.

4148 NW 13th St., 352-372-1226
sandysresale.com

92

SHOP VINTAGE
IN DOWNTOWN HIGH SPRINGS

High Springs is called the Gateway to the Springs, but it is also home to a collection of vintage and antique shops in a charming and historic downtown. The area is very walkable, so you can park the car and walk to a variety of shops, restaurants, and even a brewery. The Bird Nest and Decades on Main antique shops offer the perfect experience for treasure hunters and collectors. Unique Notions has a variety of local goods, art, and home decor. For a nostalgic sweet treat to beat the heat, check out Florida Creamery, serving up hand-dipped ice cream and more. When you've worked up a thirst, head to Colsie Coffee and Bakeshop for a latte or High Springs Brewing Company for a cold craft beer. The small-town historic charm of High Springs is the perfect backdrop for a day spent shopping for vintage treasures.

The Bird Nest
18568 High Springs Main St.
High Springs, 386-454-2200

Decades on Main
18559 High Springs Main St.
High Springs, 386-454-8525

Unique Notions
23641 W US Hwy. 27
High Springs, 352-318-5719
uniquenotions.com

Florida Creamery
23629 W US Hwy. 27
High Springs, 386-628-1662

Colsie Coffee and Bakeshop
23519 W US Hwy. 27
High Springs, 386-454-2364

High Springs Brewing Company
18562 NW 237th St.
High Springs, 386-319-1792
highspringsbrewing.com

93

DISCOVER LOCAL MAKERS
AT 108 VINE

Step into an artfully curated space of handmade goods, unique gifts, and great vibes at 108 Vine. This shop is special because it highlights products created by local Gainesville artisans. The rotating selection of items means there always will be something new every time you stop by. From stationery and home decor to body care and jewelry, there's something for everyone. Interesting vintage finds add even more to look at. There's even a dedicated kids area for items like toys and crafts. While browsing, enjoy a delicious craft espresso beverage from the coffee bar. 108 Vine baristas make all syrups in-house, and the wide selection changes seasonally. 108 Vine also frequently hosts hands-on workshops, seasonal markets, special events, and themed days. They are open 8 a.m. to 6 p.m. Monday through Saturday and 9 a.m. to 5 p.m. Sunday.

3735 W University Ave.
108vine.com

EMBRACE RETRO STYLE
AT FLASHBACKS RECYCLED FASHIONS

Flashbacks Recycled Fashions is a treasure trove of timeless fashion pieces and retro style. This boutique is home to a curated selection of vintage and secondhand clothing, jewelry, accessories, and collectibles, spanning decades of fashion history. From funky '70s prints to edgy '90s grunge, Flashbacks has something for all tastes and styles. You're sure to find something special in the ever-changing selection, whether you're hunting for a statement piece for a themed party or looking to add a touch of vintage flair to your everyday wardrobe. You also can make an appointment and bring your own gently used clothes to consign at Flashbacks. With its friendly staff, eclectic atmosphere, and vast inventory, a visit to Flashbacks Recycled Fashions is always a good time. Flashbacks is open every day from noon to 6 p.m.

220 NW 8th Ave., 352-375-3752
flashbacksrecycledfashions.com

TIP

For more vintage shopping, head a few doors down to Sunshine Records. They have a wide (and organized) selection of new and used vinyl. They carry records from all genres, so you're sure to find something you like. Great vibes, knowledgeable staff, and good prices make it worth stopping in.

220 NW 8th Ave., Ste. 70, 352-559-5895
sunshinerecordshop.com

FIND THE PERFECT GIFT
AT THE SHOPPES AT THORNEBROOK

For a delightful shopping excursion, the Shoppes at Thornebrook offers an array of boutiques, galleries, and specialty shops where unique finds await. This open-air shopping center is filled with greenery, flowers, and picnic tables, making your visit feel like a stroll through a park. Try a meal at one of the local eateries, savoring fresh and flavorful dishes. Enjoy a cocktail on the patio at Cintrón, grab a breakfast sandwich from Bageland, or indulge at Thornebrook Chocolates. Peruse the boutiques for clothing, handmade jewelry, and home goods, or treat yourself to a spa or salon appointment. See the local art at Thornebrook Gallery, shop sustainably at Life Unplastic, or search for the perfect unique gift at Malgorzata's. Many events are held in Thornebrook, including spring and fall art festivals, kids fairs, movie nights and concerts, and festive holiday events. With its inviting ambiance and many shopping and dining options, the Shoppes at Thornebrook is a delightful shopping experience for everyone!

2441 NW 43rd St.
shoppesatthornebrook.com

SHOP LOCAL
AT AUK MARKET

Don't miss the chance to shop local at The AUK Market. This inviting shop is brimming with handmade goods, local art, unique gifts, and vintage finds. The AUK Market has a big selection of greeting cards, jewelry, apothecary, and clothing, all in a beautifully curated space. Discover something new every visit with rotating products and new vendors all the time. It also hosts pop-up markets, workshops, and other special events. It's open from 11 a.m. to 6 p.m. daily except Tuesdays. There are two options for a "shop and sip" experience while browsing. Dad's Bar is a casual spot in the back of the shop to grab a quick beer or wine. Curia on the Drag, right outside, offers specialty coffees, teas, and grab-and-go pastries. They also have a food truck on-site, offering plant-based seasonal dishes.

The AUK Market
2031 NW 6th St.
theaukmarket.com

Dad's Bar
dadsbar.business.site

Curia on the Drag
2029 NW 6th St.
curiaonthedrag.com

CHECK OUT
THE SHOPS DOWNTOWN

Downtown Gainesville is a hub of shops and eateries spanning a few blocks, offering a wide range of things to do and see. From trendy fashion boutiques to specialty stores and art galleries, there's something to suit every interest. Stop into How Bazar for eclectic fashion, like vintage finds, locally crafted accessories, and unique clothing pieces. If you like music, check out Hear Again Records, which has a big selection of new and used vinyl plus a friendly and knowledgeable staff to help you find what you're looking for. Grab a delicious coffee or beverage at Wyatt's Coffee to sip on while you wander downtown. And pick up a bag of locally-roasted Resident Coffee to brew at home. For a refreshing and sweet treat, head to The Hyppo for a delicious gourmet ice pop in your choice of fruity flavors.

How Bazar
60 SW 2nd St.
352-554-4511
thehowbazar.com

Hear Again Records
201 SE 1st St., Ste. 105
352-373-1800
facebook.com/hearagainrecords

Wyatt's Coffee
202 SE 2nd Ave.
352-519-5818
wyattscoffee.com

The Hyppo
214 SE 2nd Ave.
352-727-6040
thehyppo.com

98

PICK OUT A NEW PLANT
AT SERPENTINE PLANTS + PROVISIONS

Serpentine Plants + Provisions offers a wide variety of houseplants, local goods, and even wines. This botanical haven is filled with lush greenery and unique handmade treasures. It's the perfect place to grab a gift for a loved one or a new plant for your own space. The knowledgeable staff can help give you recommendations and even transfer your new plant into a beautiful pot right there in the shop. Serpentine offers a range of artisanal pots, accessories, and botanical-inspired goods to complement your plants. A variety of other locally made products and gifts fill the store, from greeting cards to candles to vintage finds. And if you like wine, Serpentine has a wonderful, curated selection of natural wines in the shop, with wine flights available every day. Tasting events and a monthly wine club subscription provide even more fun for wine lovers.

209 NW 10th Ave., 352-451-4028
serpentineshop.com

TIP

While you're in the plaza, drop by Afternoon for a delicious brunch or coffee. This counter-service casual spot offers classic favorites with a modern twist, like BLTs, dutch babies, and egg dishes. Open Thursday through Tuesday from 9 a.m. to 3 p.m.
afternoonrestaurant.com

STROLL AROUND A HISTORIC TOWN
AT THE MCINTOSH 1890S FESTIVAL

Each fall, the oak-tree-lined streets of McIntosh's historic district are filled with vendors, handmade wares, art, live music, and antiques during the McIntosh 1890s Festival. This small town was established in the 1880s but began flourishing in the 1890s. Many of the beautifully maintained homes and buildings in the historic district are from the 1890s, hence the name of the festival. In the early days, the festival had tours of historic homes, period reenactments, and folks dressed in costume. Now going into its 50th year, the festival has grown exponentially and draws around 40,000 people annually to shop the unique treasures and admire the charming historic atmosphere. Vendor booths fill several streets around the district, making this an event where you truly could spend all day. The McIntosh 1890s Festival offers not only a fun craft festival experience, but also an opportunity for the community to come together and celebrate its heritage.

McIntosh Historic District
mcintosh1890sfestival.com

TASTE SUNSHINE
AT ISLAND GROVE WINE COMPANY

Island Grove Wine Company is a local favorite for fruit wines, highlighting Florida's homegrown berries. The winery started as a 200-acre blueberry farm in 1995 and progressed into crafting wine from extra berries in 2009. Now it is a full-fledged winery, offering over 20 varieties of fruit wines. The winery still specializes in crafting wines from their own organically grown blueberries. They also offer a vibrant selection of wines made with other fruits, often with a tropical flair. The Island Grove Winery headquarters is where the magic happens. This is where the blueberries are grown, made into wine, and finally bottled. You can tour the facility on weekdays from 10 a.m. to 4 p.m. Just a few minutes down the road, you'll find the Tasting House. This is the place to sample the fruit wines, purchase bottles to take home, and even shop for local goods and gifts.

Island Grove Wine Company Winery Facility
24703 SE 193rd Ave., Hawthorne, 352-481-9463

Island Grove Wine Company Tasting House
21848 S CR 325, Hawthorne, 352-481-1012

islandgrovewinecompany.com

TIP

Add a stop at The Orange Shop in Citra while you're in this area. They sell a variety of farm-fresh Florida citrus fruits and have been operating since 1936. This shop definitely has the feeling of an Old Florida roadside market. Make sure to snap a postcard-worthy picture with the vintage-style sign out front!

18545 N US Hwy. 301, Citra, 800-672-6439
floridaorangeshop.com

ACTIVITIES
BY SEASON

SPRING

SUMMER

FALL

WINTER

SUGGESTED ITINERARIES

DATE NIGHT

HISTORY BUFFS

ON THE WATER

OUTDOOR ADVENTURES

GATORS FANS

PLANT LOVERS

GREAT FOR KIDS

DAY TRIPS

ANIMAL LOVERS

ARTS ENTHUSIASTS

WEEKEND GETAWAYS

INDEX